2-5-2013

The Problem of HFT

*Collected Writings on
High Frequency Trading
& Stock Market Structure Reform*

Haim Bodek

Decimus Capital Markets, LLC

www.haimbodek.com

E-published in the United States. January 2013.
Published in the United States. January 2013.

ISBN-13: 978-1481978354

ISBN-10: 1481978357

For information contact:

Haim Bodek – Managing Principal

Decimus Capital Markets, LLC / Haim Bodek ConsultingSM
203-286-4470
haim@haimbodek.com
http://haimbodek.com

Table of Contents

SECURITIES EXCHANGE ACT OF 1934

Sec 6 b(5) (5): The rules of the exchange are designed to prevent fraudulent and manipulative acts and practices, to promote just and equitable principles of trade, to foster cooperation and coordination with persons engaged in regulating, clearing, settling, processing information with respect to, and facilitating transactions in securities, to remove impediments to and perfect the mechanism of a free and open market and a national market system, and, in general, to protect investors and the public interest; and are not designed to permit unfair discrimination between customers, issuers, brokers, or dealers, or to regulate by virtue of any authority conferred by this title matters not related to the purposes of this title or the administration of the exchange.

I. The Problem of HFT

Haim Bodek
Decimus Capital Markets, LLC / Haim Bodek Consulting SM
January 2013

What is the Problem of HFT?

Prior to 2009 I believed that modern high frequency trading (HFT) was simply another name for automated or electronic market making (AMM or EMM)[1], the predominant form of algorithmic liquidity providing activity present in US equity markets over the period from 2000-2007. Like most outsiders to HFT, I hadn't yet fully grasped the significance of the bifurcation of automated strategies in cash equities markets. The split had resulted in the ascendancy of a new breed of high frequency turnover scalping strategy. These inventory-neutral strategies, which focused on capturing exchange rebates on electronic exchanges running the maker-taker market model, eventually evolved into what we now know as modern HFT.

As it turns out, the practices of these "new market makers" were indeed very new, radically different from the AMM/EMM tradition. Where traditional AMM/EMM desks focused on competing for order flow and typically scaled through risk capacity in conjunction with superior quantitative pricing and risk management methods, HFTs leveraged technology and market microstructure to achieve an edge over the market. HFTs were also markedly different when it

---

[1] Scotti, M. "At the Speed of Light – Automated Market Makers Alter the Map" Traders Magazine, October 2008.
http://www.tradersmagazine.com/issues/20_287/102252-1.html?pg=1

came to how they handled risk, scaling up volumes using frequency while keeping risk exposures within highly constrained inventory limits. Unlike automated market makers, HFTs weren't focused on acquiring exclusive order flow arrangements. Instead, they focused on asserting influence over the market structure itself to accommodate the requirements of specific HFT strategies. HFTs were masters of leveraging the plumbing of electronic exchanges to get an edge. With automation, the US equities market had evolved into a vast complex machine, one that was purposefully well-tuned to the nuances of HFT scalping strategies.

Modern HFT wasn't a paradigm shift because its innovations brought new efficiencies into the marketplace. HFT was a paradigm shift because its innovations proved that anti-competitive barriers to entry could be erected in the market structure itself to preference one class of market participant above all others.[2] In practice, these barriers trumped other advantages such as captive order flow arrangements. The HFT business strategy was to work with exchange partners to align the features of the exchange with the features of the algorithmic strategies themselves. The primary goal of achieving superior queue position in the order book was the most coveted, but certainly not the only advantage sought. And, given the volume potential of these strategies and the competitive pressure that the exchange industry faced, a number of for-profit electronic exchanges determined that it was in their interest to help HFTs achieve the requisite market microstructure changes that would

---

[2] Patterson, S. and Eaglesham, J. "Exchanges Get Closer Inspection" Wall Street Journal, 19 Nov 2012.
http://online.wsj.com/article/SB10001424127887323622904578129210389143012.html

assist HFT strategies in getting an edge over the electronic crowd.

Indeed, HFTs became the dominant form of trading in the US equities markets through the assistance of the electronic exchanges themselves. In pursuit of mutual gain, the exchanges provided HFTs unfair and discriminatory advantages over public customers through a number of "innovations" released in US equities market over the last five years. The real paradigm shift that HFTs brought to US equities markets was, therefore, the construction of trading environments tailored for specific trading strategies.

"It became about meeting the needs of that specific HFT community," says a technologist who worked for several top ECNs and exchanges in the 2000s. *"...It's all about what functionality I can offer the HFT that they can take advantage of. We are going after guaranteed economics."*[3] How?

The close relationship between HFTs and electronic exchanges evolved over the past decade without sufficient regulatory oversight. It shouldn't be surprising that a dynamic evolved where HFTs rewarded exchanges that provided such "guaranteed economics" with their orders. HFTs were opportunistic traders and they demanded an edge to trade. If they didn't find a compelling enough edge at a particular exchange venue, they would trade somewhere else or stay out of the market altogether. The proliferation of market centers in the US equities marketplace provided the HFTs with many choices of venue, so they naturally directed their volume to exchanges that accommodated their needs.

Granted, electronic exchanges had been put in a tough position. REG ATS opened the US equities market to

---

[3] Patterson, S. "Dark Pools." New York: Random House, Inc., 2012. p 204.

intense competition between for-profit electronic exchanges, spurring its evolution into a highly fragmented marketplace of 13 stock exchanges and approximately 50 dark pools, all competing to attract the loyalty of order flow sources. Any exchange that attained any competitive advantage with a new product, fee structure, or market structure change would find that its competitors rapidly responded with comparable innovations or outright clones. Exchanges struggled to differentiate themselves in a manner where they could establish a compelling product that would retain and grow the volume of their most sought-after and favored high-volume clients.

The "new market makers" wanted better fee structure, volume tiering, faster order interfaces, faster price feeds, and co-location products. The exchanges competed aggressively to provide these benefits to attract HFT business. With these advantages, as well as the first wave of HFT-oriented order types, HFT strategies became much more prevalent in the market in 2005-06, and the top HFTs were able to achieve results comparable to the run rates of mid-tier market makers. But these benefits weren't enough on their own to create business units with yearly run rates in the hundreds of millions, results that characterized the top HFT firms over the last five years

To achieve the unprecedented magnitude of HFT profitability over the last five years, HFTs needed the advantages provided by HFT-oriented special order types and corresponding order matching engine features – advantages that enhanced the profitability of HFT strategies through artificial and anti-competitive means. Especially from 2007 onward – when REG NMS was introduced into the US equities markets – such features were provided to HFTs through a number of exchange "innovations" that supercharged HFT run rates. Ironically, many of the most abusive features were introduced under the pretense of complying with REG NMS, the regulatory framework of the national market system meant to protect the investing public. In practice, many such features served to assist HFTs in circumventing REG NMS, leading to a two-tier system in which HFTs benefitted from deep and deliberately crafted asymmetries in order handling treatment that advantaged special order types over the traditional order types commonly employed by the public customer.

I assert that the HFT paradigm shift did not contribute to the health of the US equities marketplace. On the contrary, the net impact of modern HFT in conjunction with the exchange practice of providing HFTs "guaranteed economics" further increased the toxicity of the electronic marketplace for market participants who did not employ HFT execution methods. The introduction of HFT-oriented special order types and related order matching engine practices for specific exchange API upgrades frequently resulted in an immediate and often severe impact upon the transaction costs associated with different classes of participants, often with HFTs benefitting at the expense of the rest of the exchange's customer base. For all practice purposes, a number of "innovations" that modified electronic exchange market structure were little more than just a means to shift economics between classes of market participants (this most certainly was the case with Direct Edge's May 2009 release of Hide Not Slide).[4] The economic impact resulting from such changes was not only measurable, but closely monitored by HFTs who employed metrics that differed dramatically from traditional Transaction Cost Analysis (TCA) employed by the

---

[4] "Direct Edge launches Hide Not Slide order"
The Trade, 28 May 2009.
http://www.thetradenews.com/news/Asset_Classes/Equities/Direct_Edge_lau
nches_Hide_Not_Slide_order.aspx

buy side. If one understood HFT scalping strategy practices and measured slippage with the same tools that HFTs employed (e.g. short-term mark-to-market measures), the adverse impact of predatory HFT could be measured precisely. When one assessed execution performance using such metrics, it was hard not to conclude that modern HFT operated in a manner that dramatically increased the adverse selection of execution of non-preferred customers in the lit markets. In practice, the HFT paradigm shift amounted to little more than opportunistic and artificially engineered skimming by preferred HFTs at the expense of the rest of the electronic crowd.

HFT was all about manipulating the rules of the game. As HFTs dominated the electronic marketplace, the national market system itself evolved into a low-latency traders' marketplace. This new marketplace was characterized by extreme asymmetries that adversely impacted the diversity of algorithmic trading strategies that could successfully operate in the marketplace. In an electronic marketplace meticulously designed to accommodate HFT strategies, HFT soon became the only game worth playing.

In hindsight, the business practices that evolved should have been expected given an environment characterized by intense competitive pressures and rife with conflicts of interest, exasperated by the odd situation where exchanges transitioned to for-profit entities while preserving their self-regulatory status. Furthermore, the structure of the US equities market stacked the odds against the electronic exchanges. Exchanges struggled to create compelling market models that could sustain large scale algorithmic trading businesses in the absence of captive retail order-flow sources. Of the many pressures aligning the interests of electronic exchanges and high volume opportunistic traders, two deserve particular mention:

Firstly, the growing practice of internalizing retail order flow off-exchange – a practice attracting the interest of a number of major investment banks – contributed to the general toxicity of the lit market as the exchanges were subjected to higher concentrations of undesirable exhaust flows.

Secondly, the proliferation of dark pools (also an area of growth encouraged by the major investment banks) cut into volumes directed to exchanges and excluded opportunistic traders.

Internalization and dark pools became a significant threat to the lit markets. Electronic trading may have killed the floor, but factors such as these made the screen increasingly toxic, creating the environment where the practice of "guaranteed economics" seemed to be a necessary evil.

The problem with HFT is not that its basic strategies are illegal or even unethical. The problem with HFT is that these strategies shouldn't work at their current scale and volume, and have only come to dominate the market through the carefully crafted advantages provided by the electronic exchanges for these specific HFT strategies – advantages such as special order types and preferred order matching engine practices. The problem with HFT is that it amounts to little more than opportunistic skimming that is only possible because HFTs have been accommodated with unfair and discriminatory advantages that assist them in getting an artificial and anti-competitive edge over public customers.

Like the SOES bandits of the 1990's and "barnacle" customer market makers of the options industry, modern HFT is an artificial industry that should long ago have been relegated to the dustbin of algorithmic trading history.

The good news is that the problem of HFT can be addressed in a straightforward manner. If the features that

7

unjustly enrich HFT profitability are eliminated from electronic exchanges, either by regulators or by industry pressure, the adverse impact of HFT activity in the market will rapidly dissipate. HFT strategies will still exist, but their role will once again be limited by their natural scale and volume.

doubt it.

Speed Matters, But Only If...

When the problem of HFT first entered the industry debate, there was one property of the new HFT tradition that really stood out. The industry perception was that HFT was all about *speed,* and HFTs made no secret about it. That didn't mean speed wasn't of critical importance to the AMM/EMM tradition that preceded HFT; it was just that HFTs emphasized speed with what could only be described as a pathological focus and for reasons that were never quite discussed in any explicit manner by the greater financial industry. *Better risk control*

The reasons why speed mattered so much remained opaque at best. And while HFTs and exchanges certainly appreciated the mechanisms through which speed had gained such significance to HFT strategies, they seemed content to keep the details out of the public dialogue.

The critical topic that was missing from the industry-wide HFT debate was the critical importance of *special order types* in low latency trading strategies employed by HFTs. By keeping this crucial topic out of the dialogue, HFTs and exchanges succeeded in keeping the core mechanisms of HFT strategies opaque to the greater investment community.

The truth about the technological arms race was that, although speed mattered, you could only reap the benefits if you knew what special order type to send and when to send it. In other words, speed was only a prerequisite. Most market participants, including extremely sophisticated traders, didn't know that the opaque practices of HFT had fundamentally changed the game, requiring that one master both speed and exchange special order types, with the latter being of far greater importance. The ascension of HFT meant that the US stock market had become almost exclusively a special order type game.

Over the period of rapid HFT volume growth, while the greater investment community was focusing on what level of investment they should put into the impossible, and ultimately secondary, task of winning the speed game, exchanges continued to propagate the myth that effective execution in an HFT-oriented marketplace was all about speed.

The exchanges had reason to propagate that myth. In the latter half of the 2000's, electronic exchanges put their resources into large-scale technology services build-outs, attempting to diversify their revenue streams. The exchanges were most interested in selling a myriad of co-location services, fast price feeds, and order routing channels to anyone who felt that their execution slippage had resulted from the "speed" issue, and generally avoided any discussion of the significance of HFT-oriented order types to assist in solving slippage issues. My direct experience was that exchange marketing departments tended to segment their customer base, differentiating between institutional clients and "short term liquidity providers." If you were an HFT, you were most likely provided entirely different marketing materials than if you were an agency broker responsible for routing institutional orders. In other words, you were either marketed unfair advantages like queue-jumping or you weren't. It was that simple.

Yes, speed mattered, but only if you knew which features mattered and how to use such features. And firms could only get access to the essential information by obtaining explicit exchange guidance from exchange contacts or, in the case of certain firms, by assisting in defining features with exchange management directly.

The Alpha in an Order Type

Over a good part of the past decade, special order types often were one of the primary topics of discussion between HFT firms and exchanges. Special order types became essential, however, in assisting HFTs' exploitation of the REG NMS regulatory framework introduced in 2007, which ironically was intended to strengthen the national market system. Exchanges introduced "innovations" such as preferential price-sliding and orders that "hide and light," which assisted HFTs in circumventing impediments introduced by REG NMS that might have otherwise constrained the growth of HFT.

Such features in themselves might have served to the benefit of institutional investors if there had not been dramatic differences in order handling treatment between different classes of order types, practices which created deep asymmetries between HFT-oriented order types and order types commonly employed by institutional investors. Instead, HFTs and exchanges undermined the very body of regulation meant to protect long-term investors from inferior executions in the highly-fragmented US equities marketplace. Currently, the bulk of modern HFT volumes are executed with HFT-oriented special order types, accounting for a significant proportion of the total US equity market volume.

In light of the growing significance of special order types since 2007, their absence from industry dialogue before 2012 is noteworthy. In fact, in the hundreds of articles, interviews, conference talks, and academic papers that addressed the topic of HFT, there was virtually no mention of the role of special order types in modern HFT until the first quarter of 2012, when regulatory scrutiny of HFT-oriented special order types became public knowledge.[5]

Over the period from 2007-2012, while an unprecedented flurry of new HFT-oriented special order types were either introduced into the marketplace or revised and updated with new features, scarcely a word was spoken about these developments in the unending HFT debate. There was, of course, no mention in industry dialogue of the importance to HFT strategies of exploiting unfair and discriminatory features embedded in special order types, features which gave HFTs preferential treatment over the public customers (and which were exploited by HFTs in combination with their speed advantage).

More specifically, these innovations resulted in a number of order matching engine practices that served to preference HFTs over the public investor:

- unfair order handling practices that permit HFTs to step ahead of investor orders in violation of price-time priority

- unfair rebooking and repositioning of investor orders that permit HFTs to flip out of toxic trades

---

[5] Gallu, J. and Mehta, N. "SEC Puts Exchanges on Notice Over Computer-Driven Trades"
Bloomberg News, 4 April 2012.
http://www.businessweek.com/news/2012-04-03/sec-puts-exchanges-on-notice-over-computer-driven-trades

- unfair conversion of investor orders eligible for *maker* rebates into unfavorable executions incurring *taker* fees

- unfair insertion of HFT intermediaries in between legitimate customer-to-customer matching

- unfair and discriminatory order handling of investor orders during sudden price movements

These order matching engine practices either currently exist or have existed on nearly every major electronic exchange. The tendency for each electronic exchange to match feature for feature with rival exchanges resulted in similar functionality across market venues. Furthermore, although the specific practices noted above are well understood by HFTs and exchanges, being central to the "guaranteed economics" arrangement afforded HFTs, these order matching engine practices are, for the most part, undocumented.

The order matching engine abuses noted above represent primary alphas that assisted HFTs in growing their volumes to dominate more than half of US equity volume, features that have made traditional order types impossible to use without being subjected to order matching engine abuses. The total economic impact and the bulk of HFT edge capture are tied to these features, in conjunction with the corresponding special order types that exploit the matching engine (order types which are noted in a later section).

For the most part, the rest of the market was focused on the wrong problem – speed. Most participants (including myself) who struggled to execute effectively on HFT-oriented exchanges assumed they were using the exchange correctly via the traditional vanilla professional order types. Most market participants just thought that they weren't fast enough to compete against HFTs.

HFTs Were Playing a New Game...

Metaphorically speaking, if the market was a chess board, HFTs were using queens, rooks, knights, and bishops. In contrast, traditional investors weren't even using pawns – they were using checkers pieces.

To take the chess metaphor further, most non-insider players didn't realize that the checkers pieces they were using had no chance against any of the chess pieces, or perhaps didn't realize that chess pieces existed at all

who's problem is THAT?

For the most part, no one thought that the problem was the game had changed and you couldn't play checkers anymore. Many reputable and quite sophisticated firms that invested in the technological arms race were in essence simply trying to play checkers faster. But if you didn't use the right pieces and play the right game, you were going to lose. You had to learn chess, and use the new pieces. There was no way around it. HFT was all about playing the right game with the right pieces, and playing it very well against the public customer who was effectively playing the wrong game with the wrong pieces.

For five long years, the greater investment community was subjected to unnecessary transaction costs as they transferred "guaranteed economics" to HFT firms and exchanges though mechanisms unbeknownst to them. As long as HFT practices remained opaque, it was so much easier to believe HFTs were simply faster than it was to admit HFTs thrived through artificial means.

Given how much press and controversy HFT has generated, it really is quite perplexing that the importance of special order types in modern HFT strategies somehow never entered the dialogue. With hundreds of papers and news articles on HFT, no one seemed to have made the connection that the bulk of US equity market volume attributed to HFT was typically executed using HFT-oriented order types and HFT-preferred API interfaces which gave HFTs an edge over less sophisticated market participants.

The order flow that came into electronic exchanges from execution service providers serving retail and institutional investors certainly wasn't executing with privileged HFT order types such as the BATS Only Post Only order type, NASDAQ's Post Only order type with automatic re-entry enabled, NYSE ARCA's Post No Preference Blind ALO order type, or Direct Edge's Hide Not Slide Post Only order type. For the most part, agency brokers weren't leveraging the various ISO order types in the correct scenarios either. HFT was and is all about these HFT-oriented order types, as well as other even more sophisticated derivatives of such order types. In fact, modern HFT would cease to be profitable without HFT-oriented order types.

When you review the industry dialogue on order types over the last five years, there are only isolated cases where the topic of advanced order types even comes up in the HFT debate. For example, ISOs are mentioned briefly in a few HFT-related articles, as are the more basic Post Only order types. However, there really isn't any documentation out there that describes why such order types matter. In fact, with regard to special order types, the most attention that any order type received was generated by the "Flash Order" controversy of 2009, an order handling phenomenon that impacted at most 1-2% of US equity volume and nearly resulted in a Flash Order ban by the SEC.[6] In comparison,

[6] Rogow, G. "Schumer Tells SEC To Curb 'Flash' Order Or He Will" MarketWatch, The Wall Street Journal, 24 July 2009.
http://www.marketwatch.com/story/schumer-tells-sec-to-curb-flash-order-or-he-will-2009-07-24

the special order type phenomena that are described here apply to the vast majority of modern HFT volumes, accounting for the majority of HFT trades that occur in the lit electronic exchanges.

To re-emphasize the point further: speed didn't help you much if your order was price-slid to the back of the queue, or routed away to hit phantom prices, or queue-jumped, or set up for what I call collisions – microstructure conditions where aggressively priced public customer orders were exposed to order handing abuses that assisted HFTs in extracting rebates. The alpha was now in the order type, overwhelming the alpha in many quantitative signals and strategies.

You either had to execute like an HFT or bleed into the market. You were either predator or prey according to extremely specific order handling treatment. There was no other choice in the lit markets. Anyone who wasn't employing the right order types in the right conditions was bleeding edge into microstructure traps corresponding to the five classes of order matching engine abuse previously mentioned.

It was imperative that one executed like an HFT if one expected to get a tolerable result. But that didn't mean you made a lot of money if you converted over to using to HFT-oriented order types and used the right techniques. If you started using HFT techniques as I recommend, it only meant you were only going to protect yourself against some of the more egregious slippages. If you thought you were going to be able to compete with the other HFTs in the highly competitive microstructure conditions relevant to HFT scalping, you probably were setting yourself up for disappointment.

Nonetheless, if you made the right changes, then overnight the lit markets would appear less toxic, for you were now eliminating a significant number of transactions that were executing in adverse conditions. Though it should be pointed out that the changes you made to protect yourself from being executed in adverse conditions often ended up making the execution job tougher. Liquidity seemed to dry up if you were using the right order types and strategies but were not fast enough to maneuver to get to the top of the queue. And yet, if you measured the reduction in your slippage, you would find that the adoption of HFT-oriented order types justified taking on the new challenges associated with utilizing the advanced features of electronic exchanges correctly.

But No One Else Wanted to Play

The "guaranteed economics" that were provided to HFTs through specialized order types tailored to HFT strategies amount to what is likely a staggering sum when one considers the sheer amount of volume executed in asymmetric conditions that transferred edge to HFT firms over the last five years. Market fragmentation in combination with the maker-taker market model, and in conjunction with a dramatic period of exchange "innovation," had resulted in a new form of artificial edge. The net result was that unfair and discriminatory asymmetries in exchange order handling had been introduced into the marketplace. Special order types were the key to unlocking the advantages.

The paradigm shift of HFT had succeeded in dramatically altering the competitive environment of the US equities marketplace. A new edge had been created for the taking, a consequence of exchange matching engine "innovations" that by design dovetailed with HFT scalping strategies. Thus a new type of market inefficiency had been introduced into the market, one that adversely impacted the public customer with the advantage landing squarely in the center of the HFT wheelhouse. None of this was by chance.

The practices of the "new market makers" as it turns out really were indeed very new, radically differing from the AMM/EMM tradition. It was about designing market structures that accommodated specific strategies. It was all about setting the rules of the game in such an asymmetric manner that HFT was the only game that could be played.

HFTs and exchanges had succeeded in stacking the deck against the institutional investors. But as the paradigm shift of HFT ran its course, and as investors lost confidence in the structure of the market itself, the equity space compressed and volumes shifted to dark pools.

In hindsight, it should be no surprise to the exchanges that the institutional investor fled to the dark pools. That is the natural consequence of unfair and discriminatory business practices that corrupted the US equities marketplace.

HFTs and exchanges had invented a new game and for a while they were winning. But by late 2012 they had learned the hard way that they had invented a game no one else wanted to play.

II. HFT Scalping Strategies

"Introduction to HFT scalping Strategies"
Haim Bodek and Mark Shaw
Decimus Capital Markets, LLC / Haim Bodek Consulting [SM]
November 2012

Originally published online:
http://haimbodek.com/research/IntroHFTScalpingStrategies.pdf

Introduction

This paper summarizes the intentions, key properties and observable effects of the particular class of high frequency trading known as HFT scalping. By using market structure advantages that have in effect circumvented the regulatory framework of Regulation NMS, HFT firms employing these strategies dominate US equity market volumes. This class of HFT trading leads to observable market phenomena such as high frequency price fluctuations, low fill-to-cancel ratios and liquidity gaps. Traditional electronic execution services and execution strategies commonly utilized by buy side equity traders often operate in a manner that is exploited by HFT scalping strategies.

HFT scalping strategies use market structure advantages to the detriment of counterparties unversed in the often undocumented nuances of exchange special order types and order matching engine logic. This paper does not directly address closely related high frequency strategies such as latency arbitrage and rebate arbitrage, though these strategies often use concepts and techniques from HFT scalping. While this paper's focus is on the US equity markets, the basic concepts of HFT scalping are applicable to financial markets in general.

High frequency trading accounts for over half of all trades and messages on the US equity exchanges.[7, 8] Many high frequency strategies, including rebate arbitrage, latency arbitrage, order anticipation, and high frequency statistical arbitrage, have origins in and/or borrow techniques from HFT scalping, which is characterized by:

High Frequency Turnover – passive scalping of a micro-spread

Queue Position – a dependence on order rank and order book depth

Low Latency – precise and timely reaction to market microstructure events

Exchange Microstructure – usage of special order types and order matching engine features

Rebate Capture – subsidized costs through "post only" orders and tiered rebates

Low Risk Tolerance – avoidance of risk and usage of market book depth to reduce risk

Basic HFT scalping originated as a simple spread capture strategy – lean on order book depth, post on the best bid/offer and flip to the other side – from the Chicago futures markets, spreading to the equities markets in the early 2000's.[9] Over time, it evolved from a straightforward flipping strategy to the HFT scalping that dominates today's US equity exchanges, where profitable rebate capture when

---

[7] Financial Stability Oversight Council. "2012 Annual Report." 18 Jul 2012. p 88. http://www.treasury.gov/initiatives/fsoc/Documents/2012%20Annual%20Report.pdf
[8] Zhang, X. F. "High-Frequency Trading, Stock Volatility, and Price Discovery." Dec 2010. p 41. http://papers.ssrn.com/sol3/papers.cfm?abstract_id=1691679
[9] Patterson, S. "Dark Pools." New York: Random House, Inc., 2012. p 52.

making a "zero width" market by buying and selling at same price is possible. Its core intent is, on every round trip trade, to step ahead of supply-and-demand imbalances evident in market depth, and to capture a micro-spread by closing on the other side for a tick or to scratch out by closing on the same side, both of which are favorably subsidized by rebate in the maker-taker market model that is currently prevalent in US equities. A prerequisite is favorable queue position: the scalper must have a high probability of entering the trade as well as a high probability of either exiting for spread (winner) or, if the winner cannot be obtained, of exiting for scratch to avoid losses. Absent a reliable prediction on what the next tick will be, this simple win-or-scratch strategy should not be profitable in a competitive, fair and orderly market, where competition for queue position and favorable execution would presumably be saturated.

To make it profitable, there must be some structural advantage (alpha) in addition to the basic order book depth asymmetry signals and execution tactics. The HFT scalpers' alpha is not a traditional prediction of market movement; it is an "effective alpha" obtained through the exploitation of market technologies (i.e. exchange "plumbing") and market microstructure. HFT scalping methods that leveraged the precursor to spam-and-cancel[10] strategies, using post only orders (order types that discriminate against order flow by trading only against marketable orders willing to pay taker fees), gradually gained market share before the adaptation of Regulation NMS in 2007. Upon the technological and microstructure changes that were introduced to the

---

[10] Bodek, H. "Locked Markets, Priority and Why HFTs Have an Advantage: Part I: Spam and Cancel." Decimus Capital Markets, LLC. Tabb Forum, 11 Oct 2012. http://haimbodek.com/research/The%20Problem%20of%20Locked%20Markets%20-%20Part%20I%20-%20whitepaper.pdf

exchanges after the adaptation of Regulation NMS in the US equities markets, HFT scalping's growth exploded.

Low latency order placement, originally a stand-alone alpha that enabled HFTs to race to the top-of-queue in a "winner-take-all" competition, is now simply a prerequisite for conducting any variant of HFT scalping strategies. Delay results in unfavorable queue position and poor execution. Colocation reduces latency, allowing HFTs to identify favorable market microstructure conditions and to respond ahead of other traders.

The sophisticated usage of special order types and order matching engines in today's US equity exchanges is now a primary alpha. The existence of undocumented features of special order types,[11, 12, 13, 14] including those that "hide and light," have become an important topic of debate and controversy in the press.[15, 16, 17] When used appropriately,

---

[11] BATS. "Display-Price Sliding."
http://batstrading.com/resources/features/bats_exchange_pricesliding.pdf
[12] Direct Edge. "Direct Edge Guide to Order Types."
http://www.directedge.com/Portals/0/docs/NextGen%20Guide%20to%20Order%20Types.pdf
[13] NASDAQ. "Protocol Quick Reference."
http://www.nasdaqtrader.com/content/ProductsServices/TRADING/Protocols_quickref.pdf
[14] NYSE Arca. "NYSE Arca Equities Order Types."
http://usequities.nyx.com/markets/nyse-arca-equities/order-types
[15] Patterson, S. and Strasburg, J. "For Superfast Stock Traders, a Way to Jump Ahead in Line." Wall Street Journal, 19 Sept 2012. A1.
http://online.wsj.com/article/SB100008723963904439892045775992436935661670.html
[16] Patterson, S. and Strasburg, J. "How 'Hide Not Slide' Orders Work." Wall Street Journal, 19 Sept 2012. A12.
http://online.wsj.com/article/SB100008723963904448127045776058402631350860.html
[17] Chapman, P. "Trading Official Says Fewer Order Types Will Help Simplify Marketplace." Traders Magazine, 9 Oct 2012.

these order types ensure favorable queue position, providing HFT with better execution as well as protection against losses. HFTs use special order types to gain favorable queue position on entry, ahead of customers and other traders. On exit, knowledge and manipulation of queue position allow HFTs to flip out for outright winners or for scratch instead of 1 tick losers. The particular mechanisms for achieving superior queue position tend to be quite different per exchange, with a variety of specific microstructure features (e.g. price-time priority corruption and conditions where internally self-locked markets are permitted) essential to getting ahead of the electronic crowd. A simple example of a "hide and light" trade is given in the Appendix.

HFT scalps micro-edges and rebates. Tiered rebates subsidize opportunity costs and realized losses, turning scratch trades into winners. Large losses due to sweeps (adverse price movements against their transient and/or potential positions) can overwhelm any profitability, so management of sweep risk is paramount. HFTs use the market microstructure to detect and avoid sweep risk, which is the risk associated with trading against large informed toxic orders (e.g. large institutional orders) that take out multiple levels of the order book. For example, HFTs are able to identify critical conditions where they are potentially exposed to toxic order flow by monitoring microstructure phenomena associated with Intermarket Sweep Orders (ISOs). By comparing the slow Stock Information Provider (SIP) feed with the faster trade and quote data from direct co-located exchange price feeds, HFTs can identify dislocations (e.g. trades printing through the SIP feed quotes) associated with sweep events. Upon detection of a

http://www.tradersmagazine.com/news/locked-markets-rule-change-110389-1.html?pg=1

possible sweep event, HFTs rapidly withdraw their liquidity to avoid interacting with the adverse flows.

Thus superior cancellation latency is key for avoiding "negative alphas" from sweeps that would otherwise result in large losses that would overwhelm any naive flipping strategy. This cancellation latency to avoid sweeps is a primary competitive dimension of HFT scalping that is not commonly discussed in academic research.

HFT scalping is predatory in its aim of stepping ahead of institutional order flows. It can be characterized as an opportunistic and discriminatory mimic of traditional market making – where HFT uses opaque advantages, including special order types, instead of explicit market making privileges – without the market making obligations. It is not a traditional spread-scalping strategy that posts on each side of the spread, relying on speed to jump ahead of the rest of the market. It is not a traditional strategy based on low latency – speed is simply a prerequisite for effective utilization of special order types and market microstructure. Unlike traditional quantitative strategies whose alphas are valuation oriented, HFT scalping is market structure oriented, tracking liquidity and exploiting exchange features to attain preferential order treatment.

Traditional high frequency quantitative strategies rely on well-known valuation-based alphas, including correlated pairs, baskets and futures signals. These traditional strategies generally require significant risk tolerance to scale up, whereas HFT scalping typically does not as it can use the market liquidity itself as insurance against large losses via its superior queue position and execution. However, quantitative strategies, along with traditional cross-product arbitrage strategies, can be and are overlaid on top of the basic HFT scalping framework to produce hybrid strategies.

Phenomena of HFT Scalping

Since 2007, adverse effects in the US equities markets have become a growing concern within the financial industry and the general media. Many forms of adverse selection, unexpected slippage and escalating transaction costs can be tied to specific features of HFT scalping practices and exchange order matching engine features. Institutional equity traders are well aware of the adverse impact of predatory HFT strategies. However, the core activity of HFT scalping strategies might be inadvertently attributed to less prevalent abuses such quote stuffing, spoofing, pinging, or more discriminatory order anticipation and "statistical front-running" models. Many of the effects are correctly attributed to HFT firms, but are byproducts of large scale HFT scalping strategies rather than primary strategies in of themselves. Examples include fluctuations in quote sizes due "spam and cancel" strategies, the observed disadvantaged fills of traditional orders typically used by smart order routers due to exchange price-sliding practices, and the observed rapid withdrawal of liquidity in today's markets that can be explained by the low risk tolerance of HFT scalping.

A major change associated with the growth of HFT strategies is the frequent occurrence of visible and dramatic rapid liquidity withdrawal on sweep-like events, commonly associated with a single tick price move. Such phenomena are especially prevalent in low-priced names saturated with HFT scalping activity such as BAC. The observed liquidity withdrawal is a byproduct of HFT's sensitivity to changes in market sizes and trades, a result of HFT scalping's dependence on queue depth and position signals. In many cases the price movement will be exasperated through a sub-millisecond withdrawal that, to institutional equity traders, can appear coordinated due to mutually understood signals that have proliferated throughout the HFT industry.

Liquidity provided by HFTs is also highly correlated with market impact since the HFTs pull out when potential sweep risk is detected. When triggered, sweep signals initiate a cascade of cancellations by HFT scalpers, resulting in a rapid loss of liquidity. Such events are also commonly associated with aggressive Immediate or Cancel (IOC) Intermarket Sweep Order (ISO) "taking" activity and aggressive Day ISO orders types being posted by the top HFT firms to set the new price.

HFT scalping is predicated on the ability to flip out, i.e. rapid turnover to avoid holding risk. This means HFT scalpers, individually and as a group, are highly risk adverse and will not hold what they perceive as potentially risky positions, and aim for high frequency turnover to neutralize unanticipated adverse flows. Unwanted risk that they enter into is rapidly flipped from one participant to another in a game of hot potato,[18] ultimately leaving the risk with whoever is too slow to get out of the way, often professional traders who are unfamiliar with HFT scalping strategies.

Because of the extremely rapid responses by HFTs to what they perceive as an unfavorable market condition, there is no time for slower market participants to replenish the market book when size is pulled by the HFTs. HFT pulling can be triggered by microstructure changes, before onset of filled trades due to sweeping activity. In some cases, quote pulling by one large HFT at the top-of-queue top-of-book can create a cascade as other HFTs interpret the rapid reduction in quantity ranked ahead of them as a trigger to pull.

---

[18] Kirilenko, A., Kyle, A. S., Samadi, M., Tuzun, T. "The Flash Crash: The Impact of High Frequency Trading on an Electronic Market." 26 May 2011. p 29.
http://papers.ssrn.com/sol3/papers.cfm?abstract_id=1686004

The HFT herd activity of rapidly canceling in these conditions can lead to further market disruption beyond the initial sweep event, a pattern seen all too often in the US equity markets where posted HFT liquidity vaporizes and the hot potato flip-out of toxic flows is triggered among HFTs.[19] Coincident HFT pulling, whether due to perceived or actual risk, drives the price through multiple levels. This leads to the now common mini-flash crash effect, where rapid liquidity withdrawal leads to a temporary liquidity void with significant disruption of the process of price discovery. In fact, HFT insiders readily admit that mini-flash crashes are an endemic problem without a clear solution:

"the mini-flash crash we do not freely talk about ... happens every day once the best price is pierced" [20]

The advantages in queue position and priority offered by the special order types have likely altered the institutional equity traders' overall perception of the equity market. These traders observe apparent market toxicity which in fact is not due to adverse order flow, but due to deep asymmetries between advantaged HFT insiders and disadvantaged institutional traders. The special order types preferred by HFT scalpers and the exploited features make it more difficult for traditional orders to get filled in the expected way. For example, undocumented "queue jumping" features[21] at the exchanges can give the appearance of "statistical front running," as traditional orders

---

[19] Madhavan, A. "Exchange-Traded Funds, Market Structure and the Flash Crash." 13 Jan 2012.
http://papers.ssrn.com/sol3/papers.cfm?abstract_id=1932925&http://papers.ssrn.com/sol3/papers.cfm?abstract_id=1932925

[20] Panel on High Frequency Trading. Sandler O'Neill 2011 Global Exchange and Brokerage Conference, 9 Jun 2011.

[21] "For Superfast Stock Traders, a Way to Jump Ahead in Line." op. cit.

fall to the back of the queue and tend to miss execution at the expected time and/or price.

Mainstream electronic trading services (execution services), including those provided by top tier investment banks, do not effectively counter HFT scalping. In fact, the services quite often inadvertently enhance HFT edge capture to the detriment of the services' institutional clients. Popular techniques to limit market impact, such as order slicing and various weighted averaging strategies, can backfire when they interact with HFT scalping strategies employing special order types and market microstructure features. For example, traditional strategies are not primarily driven by exchange microstructure conditions, which means passive orders can enter disadvantaged queue positions when submitted by these strategies. These passive orders are commonly exploited for use as "insurance" by HFT scalpers to avoid losses due to sweep events. Until recently, the concepts that drive HFT scalping have for the most part been absent from execution services and research materials provided by investment banks. It is only recently that execution services have started to focus on addressing these issues as a primary impediment to achieving fair and balanced execution performance.[22]

Summary

HFT scalping relies on superior queue position, avoidance of market sweeps, and rebate capture. Special order types and knowledge of market microstructure make alpha-less micro-spread capture a lucrative trading strategy. HFT

---

[22] e.g. Puaar, A. "SocGen enhances algos to sidestep HFT." The Trade, 18 Jul 2012.
http://thetradenews.com/newsarticle.aspx?id=9278&terms=SocGen+enhances+algos+to+sidestep+HFT

scalping's impact on the equity markets include high frequency price fluctuations, high order cancellation rates and liquidity gaps. Trading algorithms provided by traditional execution services often unnecessarily subsidize HFT scalping profits to the detriment of institutional clients.

III. Why HFTs Have an Advantage

"Locked Markets, Priority and Why HFTs Have an Advantage"
Haim Bodek and Mark Shaw
Decimus Capital Markets, LLC / Haim Bodek Consulting SM
October- November 2012

Originally published online at the Tabb Forum:
http://tabbforum.com/opinions/locked-markets-priority-and-why-hfts-have-an-advantage-part-i
http://tabbforum.com/opinions/locked-markets-priority-and-why-hfts-have-an-advantage-part-2-hide-and-light
http://tabbforum.com/opinions/why-hfts-have-an-advantage-part-3-intermarket-sweep-orders
http://tabbforum.com/opinions/why-hfts-have-an-advantage-part-4-winner-take-all-the-day-iso

Part I – Spam and Cancel

In 2005, Regulation NMS was adopted to bind U.S. equity markets into a unified national market. REG NMS was implemented market-wide in 2007, a year particularly notable as an inflection point for the rapid growth of high-frequency trading volumes. I assert that the seemingly coincidental intensification of HFT activity in 2007 is intimately related to the adoption of Rule 610 of REG NMS, which banned locked markets and which HFTs and exchanges leveraged for mutual gain.

In this series of articles, I make the case that to address the HFT problem – which is very real – we must reignite the discussion, purpose and intent of Rule 610 and the ban on locked markets. In other words, solving the problem of locked markets in a manner that is fair and non-discriminatory for all market participants will also tame the HFT problem.

HFT is about being first in the queue, period. That is an HFT's primary alpha. The implementation of REG NMS in 2007 changed the mechanisms for achieving queue position in a price-time priority market. This fundamentally changed trading strategies and exchange matching practices. By banning locked markets, REG NMS constrained the mechanisms through which a price movement occurred in the U.S. market. Thus, Rule 610 defines precisely the conditions in which an HFT can achieve a superior place in the queue (i.e., when an order would not lock an away market).

Yes, speed matters. However, the core HFT alpha can only be realized if you know what order type to send and when to send it. This process is completely dictated by how exchanges implemented REG NMS, Rule 610, order matching engine features, and very specific order types.

In theory, for a single price movement in the U.S. equities marketplace to occur, each exchange would have to show a gap of two or more ticks before a new price would be accepted on any exchange that established a more aggressive price level. With 13 exchanges, we know that HFTs are not waiting for a two-tick-wide national best bid and offer before placing their bets. Understanding this and mastering exceptions to Rule 610 became the name of the game, whether such features are adequately documented or, in many cases, not.

Prior to Rule 610; HFT scalping strategies could lock markets. Rule 610 changed the HFT game in such a significant manner that it can be thought of as a different phase of the HFT algorithmic trading tradition. The ban resulted in HFTs being forced to engage in "spam and cancel" strategies that repeatedly attempted to get to the top of the order queue on a price move. Such strategies would attempt to "step in the middle" to set a new aggressive price. This invariably locked away markets. Rule 610 demanded that such orders not be accepted at the entered price.

This activity caused immense load on exchanges, but in no way did exchanges want to discourage high-volume HFT order flow. To court HFTs, exchanges provided a number of specialized features to assist "spam and cancel" strategies, many of which are still operational today.

A common order matching engine feature that exchanges used to fulfill Rule 610 was to "price slide" the order. This practice modifies the price of an order that locked the market by, in the words of one exchange, ticking the order back in a "convenient" and "sensible" manner. When these orders were slid back, and did not have a high queue placement, the HFTs would first know that there was an order ahead in a better queue position, and second, cancel the order and retry.

While HFTs canceled their slid orders, traditional investor orders would typically just slide without being canceled. This causes the institutional orders to move to the back of the queue and away from the trading action. In this strategy, the HFTs would monopolize the top of the book, interacting with marketable orders, while the institutional-side orders would be at the bottom of the queue only to be executed when a large buyer or seller cleared the book.

To execute these spam-and-cancel strategies even more quickly, HFTs utilized specialized order confirmation information to detect being slid so they could quickly cancel the price-slid order. Exchanges also provided alternative cancel-back or "opt out" options that literally rejected orders that might have otherwise been placed in a disadvantaged queue position.

Many institutions have no idea that their orders are being slid away from the top of the book. In many instances, institutional clients and their brokers are not being adequately informed. In some instances institutions and brokers are not even receiving price-sliding information on exchange confirmations unless they specifically ask for it.

Many people believe that high cancel rates are an attempt to sniff out larger orders; however, many times it is these spam-and-cancel strategies jockeying for top-of-book status that just push institutional orders out of the way, only to trade when the market moves against them.

This is one early example of how seemingly straight-forward and appropriate order types are being leveraged not to take advantage of institutional flow, but to make institutional flow irrelevant to the point where the institutional order is disadvantaged.

This spam-and-cancel order-handling treatment is the precursor of special order types, which, for all practical purposes, exist to assist a specific type of sophisticated trader whose primary intent is to step ahead of all other customers.

In summary, Rule 610, which banned locked markets, dramatically changed microstructure to dictate when HFT scalping strategies were permitted to get to the top of queue. In practice, Rule 610 created an environment in which HFT scalping strategies needed to use a feedback loop of price-sliding information or plain rejects iteratively, sending and canceling large numbers of unexecuted transactions to get an order to "stick" at the best price at the top of an order book. Such strategies were lucrative but burdened exchanges with heavy transaction rates and canceled orders.

In the next article, we will explore how exchanges courted firms engaged in "spam and cancel" strategies by providing them specialized order types and order matching features that provided a more efficient and lucrative means of achieving superior queue position.

Part II – Hide & Light

As high-frequency trading (HFT) scalping strategies began employing "spam and cancel" strategies that dominated top-of-book trading activity,[23] exchanges realized that they could generate vast amounts of orders/fees and began aligning their focus toward serving the needs of these "new market makers." To facilitate HFT strategies and get these players to the top of queue in light of Rule 610 and its ban on locked markets, exchanges began creating a number of new special order types.

A real turning point in the development of HFT-friendly order types was the introduction of orders that would "hide and light." Where a regular order would be price-slid back a tick and lit at the slid price, these new orders would be priced to lock an away market. They would be hidden at the locking price and automatically light up once the away market was no longer locked.

The hidden price was permitted to lock an away market because it was not a displayed price and thus not considered a Protected Quotation under Regulation NMS. The hidden price was not covered by the provisions of Rule

---

[23] Bodek, Haim. "Locked Markets, Priority and Why HFTs Have an Advantage: Part I: Spam and Cancel." 11 Oct 2012. http://haimbodek.com/research.html

610 that prohibited "a pattern or practice of displaying quotations that lock or cross the protected quotations of other trading centers."[24]

In other words, HFTs could get around Rule 610 and the ban on locked markets by mastering this powerful exception that permitted the HFT to "step in the middle" and lock an away market. However, this exploitation of a clever end-around of Rule 610 presented a new problem: how to simultaneously maintain queue rank and get converted from a hidden order to a displayed order. Because hidden order types are ranked below displayed quantity according to binding exchange order precedence rules, the utility of such orders was fleeting unless a mechanism could be provided to reserve one's place at the top of the queue when the market displayed.

"Hide and light" order types solved this problem of reserving a superior queue position by, in the industry jargon, "lighting" the hidden order automatically when the order would no longer result in a violation of Rule 610 (i.e. when the away market "unlocked"). In other words, the primary advantage embedded in a "hide and light" order was its ability to transform from a hidden order into a Protected Quotation at precisely the time a market was permitted to display an aggressive price. It should come as no surprise that the power of the order type was almost purely in its ability to get an HFT to the top of the queue.

Hence, the "lighting" process became key to dictating an HFT's queue position. In essence, "lighting" is the key event in which an exchange picks the winners and losers in achieving a superior queue position.

---

[24] Securities and Exchange Commission. "Regulation NMS." 9 Jun 2005. http://www.sec.gov/rules/final/34-51808.pdf

Most institutions are not even aware of the dependence of HFT strategies on exchange "lighting" events. For several years, and including to this day, the mechanisms through which orders that "hide and light" are converted from hidden orders to be rebooked as Protected Quotations are improperly and inadequately documented.

Over the period from 2007 to 2012, the introduction of special order types that "hide and light" proceeded quite quickly, as exchanges matched each other feature for feature with intense competition for HFT order flow. NASDAQ released Price to Comply. BATS released Display-Price Sliding. NYSE ARCA released Post No Preference Blind. Direct Edge released Hide Not Slide. Such order types were repeatedly modified, usually to address specific microstructure nuances that primarily impacted HFT scalping strategies. For example, certain exchanges eventually modified the feature set of order types that "hide and light" to define the specific conditions in which such orders would interact with midpoint liquidity. Another area of modification involved the conditions in which aggressive "post-only" instances of such orders would incur taker fees instead of the intended rebate capture. Lastly, the "lighting" process itself evolved significantly on a number of exchanges.

For what might appear a relatively simple order type, the number of permutations, modifications, and microstructure features (many material elements of which remain undocumented) that were introduced over this period for orders that "hide and light" is astonishing.

It is important to note that exchanges did not mandate the use of "hide and light" orders, but the importance of such order types for those HFTs engaged in "spam and cancel" strategies was undeniable. For all practical purposes, hide and light orders existed to assist HFTs in getting to the top of queue, particularly ahead of "spam and cancel" strategies.

BATS, being particularly aggressive with the adoption of special order types that "hide and light," summed up quite elegantly the appeal of such order types: "Display-Price Sliding eliminates the need for traders to retry orders multiple times in rapid succession trying to be high in priority at the next NBBO price."[25]

Where was the institutional client in all of this? For institutions using default exchange modes that subjected their orders to traditional price-sliding, they remained placed a tick back at the back of the queue away from the trading action. Even institutions that utilized orders that "hide and light" intentionally or as a default option – but that were not versed in the special relationship between Rule 610, the processing of the SIP feed, exchange order matching engine practices, and the special order types themselves – were unlikely to send orders in the appropriate usage conditions. In fact, HFTs themselves did not think institutional order flow had a competitive stake in the game at all. They thought of the battle as HFT vs. HFT. And they were right. Yes, speed matters – but only if you know what order type to send and when to send it.

In summary, to address the ban on locked markets, exchanges provided special order types that would "hide and light" orders. These order types were not mandated by exchanges, but appealed to high-speed traders formerly engaged in "spam and cancel" strategies. While HFTs employing "hide and light" order types faced off against older "spam and cancel" strategies, the institutional investor had become even more sidelined by an HFT-oriented market

---

[25] BATS. "Display-Price Sliding." 2011.
http://www.batstrading.com/resources/features/bats_exchange_pricesliding.pdf

structure, unable to effectively participate in the trading action.

Part III – Intermarket Sweep Orders

Rule 611 of Regulation NMS is called the Order Protection Rule, more commonly known as the "trade-through rule."[26]   Its goal is to prevent orders on one exchange from being executed at prices that are inferior to those of "protected" quotes at another exchange. This rule forces exchanges either to reject marketable orders or to route them to the exchange displaying the best price. In conjunction with Reg NMS Rule 610, Rule 611 provides a key protection that prohibits exchanges from executing trades that can be filled at better prices at away markets, a crucial property for binding markets in a single, unified national best bid and offer.

In theory, this rule should help investors get the best price in the market, regardless of where an order initially is routed. In practice, however, high-frequency traders have undermined the ability of others to secure the best price by exploiting an increasingly fragmented market.

In 2005, when the Reg NMS framework was being developed, decimalization in the U.S. equity markets had already resulted in a thinning of size available at the top of book, a general reduction in available market depth, and the deployment of sophisticated broker routing technologies to trade across the fragmented U.S. equities marketplace. With the threat of impending trade-through regulation, institutional traders were understandably concerned that Rule 611 would interfere with a broker's ability to serve an

---

[26] Securities and Exchange Commission. "Regulation NMS." 9 Jun 2005. http://www.sec.gov/rules/final/34-51808.pdf

institutional investor when trading in parallel across execution venues as exchanges attempted to fulfill their trade-through requirements across a fragmented marketplace. The problem is that if the client needs to access liquidity across all markets instantaneously but is prevented from doing so, the market impact of the trade could lead to rapid withdrawal of liquidity by market makers and/or situations in which the broker is unnecessarily forced to chase liquidity with orders that are denied by exchanges in an effort to comply with Rule 611. In fact, the resulting race conditions between market centers create technological pandemonium in the price feed that frequently interferes with access to instantaneous liquidity by institutional investors in a variety of conditions.

To satisfy these concerns, the SEC carved out an exemption to Rule 611, providing a special exception – the Intermarket Sweep Order (ISO) – for institutions that need to sweep through multiple levels of the order book. To quote the filing: "The intermarket sweep exception enables trading centers that receive sweep orders to execute those orders immediately, without waiting for better-priced quotations in other markets to be updated."[27]

While normal orders routed to a venue not displaying the best price would create a trade-through and force an exchange either to reject or to reroute an order, ISOs are executed without any requirement to check away market pricing or to apply trade-through protections. The stipulation to using ISO orders is that the broker-dealer is required to access all Protected Quotations across all markets that are covered by the trade-through rule and to assume all liability for compliance with Rule 611. In other words, to use an ISO order, broker-dealers need to trade across all protected

---

[27] "Regulation NMS." op. cit.

trading venues and absorb liability for the exchanges' trade-through compliance requirements.

While ISOs are meant for large institutions sweeping through the book, in practice they are really leveraged by HFTs and sophisticated proprietary trading desks to get ahead of slow Stock Information Provider (SIP) data feeds during price moves. Especially in the early period, very few broker-dealers recognized the importance of using ISOs as a primary order type for smart order routing to protect against the adverse impact of slow SIP feeds. In fact, due to liability concerns of broker-dealers, even sophisticated Direct Market Access (DMA) customers that wanted to use ISOs often were not permitted to use them, a constraint that continues to impact smaller HFTs this day. Thus the competitive dimension of ISO activity was and is constrained to a subset of HFTs when compared with the much more widespread use of orders that "hide and light."[28]

The simplest form of ISO is the Immediate-or-Cancel (IOC) ISO. This class of ISO order instructs the exchange either to immediately execute an order at a specific price or to cancel it, with no requirement to check if the order trades-through any "protected" quotation at an away exchange. To use an IOC ISO, a broker-dealer needs to affirm that it is also sending orders to any market showing a more advantageous price. The trade-through test, however, is not dictated exclusively by the slower aggregated SIP feed; if a broker has a faster direct feed, it can limit the cases in which it has to send orders to hit SIP prices that, given the fast nature of U.S. equity liquidity provisioning, in many instances are stale and no longer exist.

---

[28] Bodek, Haim. "Locked Markets, Priority and Why HFTs Have an Advantage: Part II: Hide & Light." Decimus Capital Markets, LLC. Tabb Forum, 16 Oct 2012. http://haimbodek.com/research/The%20Problem%20of%20Locked%20Markets%20-%20Part%20II%20-%20whitepaper.pdf

When the SIP feed slows down (which can happen in a fast market as a result of delays on as few as one of the thirteen exchanges), customers that use traditional orders can be disadvantaged, as they are rejected or unsuccessfully rerouted due to phantom SIP quotes created by race conditions and latencies. HFTs and other sophisticated participants that are able to use IOC ISOs suffer no such burden. In other words, while traditional orders based upon slow SIP data and trade-through routing chase SIP quotes that don't exist, HFTs using ISO orders and fast data feeds can access rapidly diminishing liquidity on price moves and thus outflank the latency-prone tactics.

In fast markets, HFTs benefit from the slow SIP feed in a manner that may exasperate rapid price movement as they maneuver to avoid adverse flows – they are able to pull their unexecuted orders on venues before they trade against customers using marketable non-ISO orders that are rerouted or rejected due to phantom SIP prices. Thus, for a portion of order flow, HFT scalping strategies are in essence protected by the exchanges' implementations of Rule 611 – implementations that in effect provide a shield against an onrush of public orders in fast market conditions, as such orders are rejected or rerouted.

The impact of the widespread use of ISOs upon the marketplace, the potential for significant price dislocation associated with "sweep events," and the problem of "phantom liquidity" have far-ranging repercussions, as discussed in BlackRock Managing Director Ananth Madhaven's excellent paper relating the use of ISOs and the relation to the flash crash.[29]

---

[29] Madhaven, Ananth. "Exchange-Traded Funds, Market Structure and the Flash Crash." 13 Jan 2012.

In summary, brokers unfamiliar with the necessity and nuances of accessing HFT-oriented markets with ISOs in fast moving markets limit the liquidity available to their clients and leave many orders unfilled, a practice that effectively shields HFTs from toxic marketable order flows and subsidizes the profits of HFT scalping strategies.

Part IV – The DAY ISO: Winner Take All

Rule 611 of Regulation NMS, also known as the Order Protection Rule, introduced Intermarket Sweep Orders (ISOs) – e.g., the Immediate or Cancel (IOC) ISO – that provide institutions a means to comply with trade-through rules while executing large orders that need to sweep through multiple levels of the order book across multiple market centers. However, as previously discussed, high speed traders leverage ISOs for another reason: to get an edge over less sophisticated traders in fast moving markets, particularly those traders who rely on exchange mechanisms for compliance with Rule 611, mechanisms that expose orders to the adverse effects of slow Stock Information Provider (SIP) data feeds.[30]

In addition to defining IOC ISOs, Rule 611 also introduced another ISO variant – the seemingly non-controversial DAY ISO order type. In fact, the DAY ISO is anything but innocuous; rather, it is an essential HFT-oriented order type packed with advantages.

---

http://papers.ssrn.com/sol3/papers.cfm?abstract_id=1932925&http://papers.ssrn.com/sol3/papers.cfm?abstract_id=1932925

[30] Bodek, Haim. "Locked Markets, Priority and Why HFTs Have an Advantage: Part III: Intermarket Sweep Orders." Decimus Capital Markets, LLC. Tabb Forum, 29 Oct 2012.
http://haimbodek.com/research/The%20Problem%20of%20Locked%20Markets%20-%20Part%20III%20-%20whitepaper.pdf

As with the case of IOC ISOs, high speed traders employing DAY ISOs can gain access to prices that would normally be inaccessible to traders who rely on exchanges to comply with trade-through rules. The DAY ISO, however, combines all the advantages of IOC ISOs with powerful features that HFTs exploit to book orders at the top-of-queue, capabilities that in fact trump the capabilities of most other HFT-oriented order types.

Originally, the DAY ISO was intended for institutions that wanted to sweep to a particular price level and then post at the best price – for example, clear the offer, then bid aggressively for more at the old offer price (buy all you can at the offer, then post a limit to buy the remainder at the old offer price). To use a DAY ISO, a broker-dealer is required either (a) to show it isn't locking or crossing away markets or (b) to sweep markets displaying prices it would otherwise lock or cross. Thus the DAY ISO order addresses conditions in which Regulation NMS puts constraints upon an order to simultaneously satisfy the ban on locked markets stipulated by Rule 610 and the trade-through rule stipulated by Rule 611.

However, the DAY ISO also provides a way to step ahead of orders that are already resting on the book – orders that were originally submitted at the same price, but were price-slid or hidden to comply with Rule 610 and the ban on locked markets. This advantage – the remarkable ability to step ahead of orders resting on the book at the same price – gives DAY ISOs a unique edge over the bulk of order types, including orders that "hide and light."[31]

---

[31] Bodek, Haim. "Locked Markets, Priority and Why HFTs Have an Advantage: Part II: Hide & Light." Decimus Capital Markets, LLC. Tabb Forum, 16 Oct 2012.

Like orders that "hide and light," the DAY ISO can be used by HFTs to lock away markets that are in fact stale phantom prices on the SIP feed that are no longer present on the away exchange. Unlike "hide and light" orders, the DAY ISO enters the market as a protected quotation and is eligible for immediate display on the book, whereas the "hide and light" order must remain in a hidden state until the away market unlocks. When sending a DAY ISO in such conditions, the burden of liability is on the HFT to demonstrate that the direct feeds used indeed show that away markets have truly faded, and that there isn't a pattern of locking protected quotations on away markets or any violation of Rule 610. If, for any reason, an HFT desires to lock an away market that displays a firm quotation (and not a phantom quotation) with a DAY ISO, the HFT would also have to take out the away market with an ISO. The other option in such a scenario would be to simply use a "hide and light" order.

DAY ISOs, like "hide and light" orders, avoid conditions that would normally result in rejection, rerouting, or disadvantaged price-sliding of aggressive orders – unfavorable order treatment that typically occurs when an exchange employs a slow SIP feed to assert compliance with the ban on locked markets and the trade-through rule. Not only do HFTs exploit DAY ISOs to get ahead of slow SIP feeds while avoiding the disadvantaged exchange order handling treatment described above, HFTs also use DAY ISOs to step ahead of "hide and light" orders already resting on the book. What is most remarkable about DAY ISOs is

http://haimbodek.com/research/The%20Problem%20of%20Locked%20
Markets%20-%20Part%20II%20-%20whitepaper.pdf

this ability to queue jump orders that arrived at the exchange at the same price as, but prior in time to, the DAY ISO.[32]

To appreciate the significance of DAY ISO queue jumping, it is key to understand that among all the special order types, only the DAY ISO can light a new aggressive price on an exchange that locks an away market. In practice, this lighting capability provides an alternative end-around to Rule 610 and the ban on locked markets and provides HFTs a backdoor to the top-of-queue.

Lighting an aggressive price with DAY ISOs is a winner-take-all sport. The first DAY ISO that arrives to set a new NBBO will light the new price when it is booked. The new price will be displayed whether or not the order is locking an away market. HFTs often leverage DAY ISOs to get to the top-of-queue on an NBBO change in cases where there is a slow SIP or when there are race conditions between prices disseminated on direct feeds. Hence, the fastest firm gets the top-of-queue and controls the actual "lighting of the market." Indeed, HFTs are dictating the timing of an NBBO change on the SIP when using DAY ISOs.

After the DAY ISO is lit, all such "hide and light" orders that were resting on the book are then displayed, triggered by the ISO lighting event. It needs to be clarified that DAY ISOs, due to their status as protected quotations, are ranked ahead of all "hide and light" orders that exist in the subordinate hidden state at the same price. Thus DAY ISOs have the special ability to step ahead (i.e., queue jump)

---

32 For another example of price-time priority corruption, where orders that "hide and light" are permitted to queue jump orders commonly used by institutional investors, see "For Superfast Stock Traders, a Way to Jump Ahead in Line."
http://online.wsj.com/article/SB10000872396390443989204577599243693561670.html

orders that previously arrived at the exchange and were resting on the book in a hidden state.

What about the case when two DAY ISOs are sent by competing HFTs? In this case, the second ISO coming into an exchange would fall behind all such lit orders, including "hide and light" orders that were queue jumped, even if the second DAY ISO arrived only microseconds later. Hence, when there is HFT competition to light a new price with a DAY ISO, second place really is the end of the line (back-of-queue). Especially in highly competitive and actively traded names, the HFT might as well cancel any DAY ISOs that fail to light the market rather than be posted at the back-of-queue.

In summary, DAY ISOs were originally intended for large institutions that needed to sweep the book and post unfilled quantity at their most aggressive price. However, such orders became the mainstay of HFTs, which use them to post liquidity ahead of slow SIP feeds in order to light aggressive new prices. DAY ISOs assist HFTs in gaining a favorable queue position by queue jumping ahead of orders that "hide and light" as well as order types commonly used by institutional investors. Execution service providers that route aggressive orders to HFT-oriented exchanges yet fail to effectively utilize the primary features provided by such exchanges in the correct usage cases, including the appropriate usage of DAY ISOs and "hide and light" orders, are unnecessarily subsidizing HFT scalping strategies and disadvantaging their customers.

IV. HFT – A Systemic Issue

Haim Bodek
Decimus Capital Markets, LLC / Haim Bodek Consulting SM
January 2013

Did An Entire Industry Fail to Do Its Homework?

How did the financial industry miss the critical point that HFTs leveraged specific order types and exchange features to generate their unprecedented volumes and returns? According to some stakeholders, it was because the bulk of market participants in the US equities marketplace had failed to put the efforts into using the features of the exchanges correctly. At least some electronic exchanges would argue that we didn't do our homework, and this view has its sympathizers, as noted by Herbert Lash in an article from October 2012:

Exchange officials deny [special order types] serve special interests, noting the Securities and Exchange Commission approves all new order types. The exchanges answer critics by saying some traders have figured out how order types can work to their advantage while other traders have failed to do their homework.

A source at the SEC said the most sophisticated exchange users go to great pains to figure order types out. Even if some may benefit certain participants more than others, "I don't know that there's necessarily fire there," the source said.

But critics say the confusion from order types allows only a few investors to profit from the changes.[33]

Though the article readily admits that special order types may play a significant role in execution performance, and in no way does it deny that special order types are a key ingredient in the profitability of HFT firms, the takeaway is that the fault, if any, lies with the firms that failed to use the exchange feature sets correctly. According to this logic, the burden of responsibility to use order types appropriately lies solely with agency brokers and their institutional investor clients.

At the September 2012 Senate hearing on Computerized Trading conducted by Senators Reed and Crapo, the issue of special order type usage was raised again. They again concluded that if professional traders were hurt because they didn't employ the appropriate special order types, then these traders were, perhaps, to blame for failing to keep up with the rules.

So, it appears that the burden of responsibility may fall on sell-side brokers and their buy-side clients in protecting themselves against predatory and abusive HFT practices on HFT-oriented market centers. Exchanges and HFTs would indeed like to shift the liability for these investor losses onto sell-side brokers and their buy-side clients by establishing that such firms were negligent in developing adequate competencies in the appropriate use of exchange features commonly exploited by HFTs. The sell-side brokers and their buy-side clients, however, do not deserve the blame. They are victims of opaque HFT practices exploiting information about features that exchanges had provided preferred HFT

---

[33] http://www.foxbusiness.com/news/2012/10/19/analysis-complaints-rise-over-complex-us-stock-orders/#ixzz2HbAopI1x

customers in an exclusive and nonpublic manner. Furthermore, if the exchanges and HFTs are successful in shifting the blame, the situation could evolve into something quite damaging to the industry as a whole by further eroding investor confidence in the broader financial system.

It is important to emphasize at this point that not even the most sophisticated user would have been able to determine how top HFT firms employed special order types by scrutinizing exchange API manuals and regulatory filings. The most important details (e.g. intended usage cases, intended order interaction sequences, order precedence rules, etc.) are not documented in any adequate manner. The lack of documentation might have been an excusable situation if such features were not commonly discussed between HFT firms and electronic exchanges in a nonpublic and exclusive manner.

For example, "spam and cancel" techniques have long been accommodated by electronic exchanges, but they are not explicitly described in exchange documentation. If such techniques could be deciphered from exchange documentation, the practices would surely be prevalent across major investment banks by now.

Another example of an exclusive HFT technique, queue jumping, is a key undocumented feature that advantages HFTs through the corruption of price-time priority. The undocumented feature of queue jumping either currently operates or has operated at every major electronic exchange in some capacity, and was routinely marketed to HFT firms by a number of electronic exchanges.

The more one studies the exchange documentation, in fact, the more apparent is our dependency on the discretion of the exchanges to inform individual customers of the features that have material impact on execution performance and the intended usage scenarios of such features.

Regardless, and given the potential for faulting the uninformed investor, it is prudent at this point for institutions not yet experienced in the use of special order types to take advantage of the recent release of information on HFT-oriented exchange features, such as the order type materials recently prepared by NASDAQ. Such firms should select an ultra-low-latency broker to assist them in leveraging such information in order to execute appropriately on HFT-oriented market centers.

What Is Being Done About HFT?

That the HFT industry started to compress in the second half of 2012 is a particularly promising development. Though this decrease is largely driven by reductions in overall market volume, it is also very likely to have been impacted by the positive changes to the market structure that have occurred over the last year.

In fact, there is reason to believe the peak of HFT dominance has passed and the HFT industry is on the wane. When one reviews market structure changes in the last year, one might note that a number of egregious practices appear to have been eliminated from the exchanges. Specific cases include normalization of binary and FIX protocols, prohibition of queue jumping on orders that "hide and light," and the levying of taker fees for aggressively priced Post Only orders. Whether these changes and others were pushed by regulators or if exchanges were acting defensively is unclear to me. All I know is that 2012 is the first year we saw the artificial industry of HFT slowly cleaned up.

Note however that my analysis of these changes has led me to the conclusion that the institutional investor is not off the hook in the short, and perhaps long, term. The market isn't getting less complex, and some of these investor-friendly changes require appropriate configuration or revisions to execution strategy to gain the intended benefits. As the issues of exchange order handling continue to be reviewed, I expect to see additional pressures on execution service providers to demonstrate greater competency for fulfilling best execution fiduciary duties using the advanced exchange features.

I should also note that it is also encouraging to see additional regulatory scrutiny of dark pools, where latency arbitrage and other abusive practices adversely impact investors in a manner that undermines the integrity of the national best bid and offer. Hopefully, the firms engaged in these practices will be held responsible.

If you listen carefully to the dialogue of the September and December 2012 Senate hearings on market structure, the implication is that the stage is being set for market structure reforms that are perhaps already underway. My perspective on what I believe has been achieved follows. (Again, this was underreported by the financial press.)

- Some exchanges, not all, have been quietly cleaning up since October 2011.

- Some of the more egregious HFT-oriented features appear to have been neutralized through order matching engine modifications.

- Certain HFTs and exchanges are admitting that they no longer have the cozy relationships they once had – this was certainly the case by second quarter 2012 when regulatory scrutiny was heating up.

- Certain electronic exchanges are on the path to becoming more open, transparent, better documented, and less exclusive. NASDAQ's recent move to provide order type documentation certainly attests to this fact.

- The concept of SRO status of for-profit exchanges appears to be under scrutiny. At the bare minimum, exchanges are certain to be subjected to a higher level of regulatory oversight going forward.

- There appears to be some degree of industry consensus and perhaps regulatory consensus that HFT-oriented electronic exchanges went too far and full market reform is likely untenable (i.e., we can't back everything out and need to make compromises).

- It appears more of the onus will be on sell-side brokers and buy-side clients to appropriately make use of exchange features, especially in light of the positive changes that have already been made to market structure.

- Regulation NMS itself is likely to become the center point of the HFT debate as 2013 progresses. REG NMS Rule 610, its ban on locked markets and its adequacy in serving long-term investors is a topic that is intermittently discussed and I hope draws more attention.

The market structure changes that are in play are definitely a moving target and overall are not likely to lead to what a true market structure reform advocate would desire. I don't see a situation where the market is truly fixed. I see a number of compromises slowly playing out that result in a better market, where egregious asymmetries are eliminated and some semblance of normalcy is returned. It isn't the preferable result, but perhaps is the most practical way forward. We should all hope that the proverbial winds of change are blowing in the right direction.

Where Do We Go From Here?

After looking at the major industry segments in the chain (HFTs, exchanges, buy-side, sell-side), and seeing how each segment adapted to the current controversy about special order types, market complexity, and unfair and discriminatory practices at the exchanges, it is clear to me that we have a systemic issue in the US equities marketplace that has delayed meaningful reforms that might have otherwise been initiated by the industry. All the groups I have noted are in some manner responsible for preserving the status quo. Based on my assessment of the situation, I made the following forecasts a few months back:

1. Regulators – We will see regulators strengthen the regulatory oversight of self-regulating exchanges.

2. Exchanges – We will see exchanges eliminate discriminatory practices and enhance their level of disclosure.

3. HFTs – We will see HFTs lose advantages and a new emphasis by such firms on market making status and order flow relationships.

4. Sell Side – We will see electronic trading desks utilize sophisticated features of exchanges appropriately.

5. Buy Side – We will see institutional investors take more responsibility for their execution performance.

In the past three months, we have indeed witnessed some very interesting developments.

- HFT giants such as Virtu and Getco have sought to diversify by emphasizing order flow sources and traditional automated market making, as indicated by their competitive bids to acquire Knight Capital.[34]

- NASDAQ has provided comprehensive materials on their order types specifically to allay concerns of unfair asymmetries in special order types.[35]

- BATS and Direct Edge have performed a number of rigorous tests on their respective order matching engines, finding and correcting issues, as well as being forthright about the adverse impact of software errors on investors.[36]

I find these developments encouraging. It is consistent with the view that modern HFT no longer has a stranglehold on the industry, and the ecosystem is in the process of changing. But we still have a long way to go.

I do have a straw-man metric for normalcy. When HFT volume collapses back down to 20% or so, we will likely have a functional market. I don't see the goal to be completely eliminating asymmetries from the market. I see the goal to be eliminating egregious advantages and abuses,

---

[34] Schmerken, I. "Getco, Virtu Pursuit of Knight Signals Consolidation Trend"
Advanced Trading, 29 Nov 2012.
http://www.advancedtrading.com/infrastructure/getco-virtu-pursuit-of-knight-signals-co/240142890

[35] Steinert-Threlkeld, T. "Nasdaq OMX Circulating Order Type Breakout"
Traders Magazine Online News, 30 Nov 2012.
http://www.tradersmagazine.com/news/nasdaq-omx-circulating-order-type-breakout-110587-1.html

[36] Patterson, S. "SEC Concerned About Other Exchanges"
Wall Street Journal, 10 Jan 2012.
http://online.wsj.com/article/SB10001424127887323442804578233803900538838.html

while providing significantly more transparency to the marketplace. The aim should be to restore a true diversity to the marketplace by eliminating artificial edges, an aim which I believe is a critical part to restoring investor confidence in the market itself.

Lastly, I want to emphasize the importance of reassessing the adequacy of Rule 610 of REG NMS and its ban on locked markets in serving long-term investors. Many of the asymmetries currently operating in US equity markets are in some manner related to how exchanges implement, manage, and comply with the ban on locked markets, but in practice allow HFTs to circumvent the undesirable constraints REG NMS places upon their strategies.

Interestingly, there appears to unanimity of views regarding a potential repeal of the ban on locked markets on both the pro and con side of the HFT debate, shared among many leaders in the industry, including individuals working at HFTs, investment banks, and exchanges, as well as well-respected market structure experts, and market reform advocates. Most agree that the ban on locked markets has produced unintended side effects that have been damaging to the electronic marketplace and which warrant reassessment. These insiders often express a sentiment such as: "Wouldn't most of the problems go away if we just repealed the ban on locked markets (returning to the situation that existed in 2006)?" And the answer is yes, with the stipulation that some of the nuances of order handling treatment might need to be further constrained should a repeal of the ban on locked markets be considered.

Regardless, I would like to see a reassessment of Rule 610 and the ban on locked markets more extensively discussed by the industry and regulators over the coming year.

V. Electronic Liquidity Strategy

Haim Bodek and Mark Shaw
Decimus Capital Markets, LLC / Haim Bodek Consulting SM
December 2012

Introduction

This paper provides an overview of Electronic Liquidity Strategy (ELS), a hybrid electronic trading approach for institutional investors that serves to assist in fulfilling best execution fiduciary duties in the heavily fragmented US electronic marketplace. ELS is a necessary outcome of electronic exchange practices that have accommodated high frequency traders and upstairs internalization units to the detriment of the public customer.

By embedding algorithmic trading strategies commonly employed by short-term liquidity providers into institutional electronic trading services, ELS aims to enhance access to available liquidity, to reduce slippage due to adverse selection, and to lower direct transaction costs. The intent of ELS is to assist large-volume institutional investors to directly compete for order flow traded by short-term liquidity providers, such as high frequency traders and upstairs internalization desks.

Electronic Liquidity Strategy

Electronic Liquidity Strategy (ELS) is the application of algorithmic trading strategies, order placement methods, and electronic market access mechanisms traditionally employed by short-term liquidity providers, in order to achieve superior execution performance for institutional trading. ELS operates under the assumption that transaction costs measured under traditional transaction cost analysis (TCA) can be reduced by capturing a micro-spread in an opportunistic and discriminatory manner that is similar to how many classes of short-term liquidity providers currently operate. By subsidizing execution performance with micro-spread capture, favorable fee treatment, elimination of adverse selection, and access to fleeting liquidity, ELS aims to reduce realized transaction costs.

ELS differs from traditional execution strategies, including passive posting strategies that aim to capture a market making spread, in that it aims to mimic active liquidity-oriented strategies currently utilized by high frequency traders (HFTs), many of which are opportunistic and predatory in nature. Active liquidity-oriented strategies often post aggressive prices in "collision" conditions to trade against participants who are slower to react to information changes in the marketplace. Active strategies provide an effective means to eliminate adverse selection by enhancing access to liquidity that is typically traded by short-term liquidity providers employing opportunistic and discriminatory tactics.

ELS is a hybrid strategy that blends the core competencies of short-term liquidity providers, such as high frequency traders and upstairs internalization units, with a traditional execution services function in order to improve total execution performance. ELS benefits from leveraging high frequency trading strategies, order placement techniques, microstructure-oriented signals, and exchange features that have become central to the competitive interaction between sophisticated market participants in today's highly fragmented US equities marketplace.

Key Differentiators of ELS

ELS emphasizes techniques and metrics that are central to the activities of short-term liquidity providers. ELS focuses on execution performance on an order-by-order basis, seeking to achieve superior post-trade metrics over short-term intervals which effectively correspond to a form of price improvement, while seeking neutral post-trade metrics over longer intervals (i.e. minimal market impact). ELS emphasizes a number of functional areas typically underutilized by traditional electronic trading services.

Signal Based Execution

ELS utilizes HFT-oriented market microstructure signals to dictate order placement. Execution decisions are triggered by market microstructure events that align opportunistically in the favor of the desired trading intention. While concepts such as time-slicing and implementation shortfall (IS) are embedded in ELS, these concepts serve to dictate the target risk exposures and not the precise timing of order placement strategies.

Opportunistic Trading

ELS attempts to "trade for edge" in a manner comparable to the strategies often employed by short-term liquidity providers. Hence, ELS may operate in a manner that is perceived as toxic or informed when opportunistically sourcing liquidity from short-term liquidity providers. For example, ELS targets conditions where it can trade at favorable prices against such liquidity providers by aggressively taking diminishing liquidity and/or posting liquidity in "collision" conditions that result in an effective edge capture from participants that are too slow to pull orders.

Exchange Features

ELS utilizes advanced capabilities offered by the US equities exchanges, including low latency price feeds, special order types, and sophisticated usage of order status acknowledgements. ELS strategies are tuned to the particular nuances of exchange market structure, especially with regard to order precedence rules that impact execution priority.

Low-Latency

Due to the transient nature of the market microstructure signals, the short-lived window of opportunity to trade at favorable prices, and the competition with short-term liquidity providers, ELS techniques necessitate direct market access capabilities provided by ultra-low latency brokers.

Market Structure and Regulatory Arbitrage

ELS can take advantage of specialized exchange features and benefits typically exploited by short-term liquidity providers – advantages that are usually only available to members of the exchange or to certain classes of participants. An example is the usage of Intermarket Sweep Order (ISO), an advantaged order type typically available only to broker-dealer members. Another example is the superior maker-taker fee structure associated with exchange members eligible for the superior fee/rebate rates associated with the highest customer volume tiers. Note that a number of ultra-low latency brokers have structured their services such that they are able provide these benefits to sponsored access customers.

Order Flow Discrimination

Firms employing ELS will focus on venue toxicity and identifiable conditions in which adverse order flows materialize in such venues. Thus an important ongoing area of research and development central to ELS is the identification of signatures associated with short-term adverse selection bias. An example signature might include identification of a liquidity sourcer that aggressively posts near-simultaneously across multiple venues. Another example might be the identification of pinging activity in dark pools that exposes orders to information leakage. In the ideal scenario, users of ELS will seek to benefit from entering into creative order flow relationships that will provide access to more diverse order sources and the opportunity to execute against less informed counterparties.

Smart Order Routing

ELS improves upon traditional order routing services by using order types commonly preferred by short-term liquidity providers (e.g. ISOs, Post Only, order types that "hide and light," etc.). ELS aims to assign a valuation or utility that can be used to rank conditions for optimal placement of orders across competing electronic venues, intelligently incorporating fee structure differentials across market venues.

Liquidity-Oriented Approach

ELS can execute on liquidity-oriented signals, where the market microstructure itself implies a change in the supply-demand balance of active market participants. ELS is systematically aggressive when liquidity is scarce and opportunistic when liquidity is abundant. ELS differs from traditional execution strategies in its emphasis of discriminatory execution tactics over passive posting strategies when executing in an opportunistic manner.

Market Impact

ELS can mask liquidity sourcing activity in microstructure conditions that are often saturated with the trading activity of opportunistic traders. When used appropriately, order placement in "collision" events where liquidity demander and provider attribution is uncertain can reduce the liquidity sourcing footprint exploited by many short-term trading strategies. In addition, certain passive conditions of interaction with order flows can be used to mask market impact. An example would be passive posting strategies in market venues that provide access to "exhaust" order flows that are commonly used by upstairs market makers to offload risk from internalization activity.

Two-Sided Liquidity Provision

ELS can enhance execution quality by utilizing two-sided opportunistic edge capture strategies typically employed by high frequency traders. The sophisticated usage of two-sided liquidity provision strategies, in concert with a means to target a cumulative risk exposure, can mask order placement activity that would otherwise result in one-sided market impact.

Furthermore, two-sided strategies are often important tools in eliminating adverse selection bias from the distribution of executed transactions as measured on a post-trade metric, in effect subsidizing the reduction of transaction costs through edge capture. ELS does *not* provide two-side liquidity by scalping a traditional market making spread, but instead responds to adverse order flows by exiting inventory opportunistically. In such conditions, ELS will aim to exit inventory for a rebate credit often at an identical price to that originally executed, a practice that assists in generating neutral post-trade metrics and which is comparable to strategies employed by short-term liquidity providers. Thus when trading against adverse order flows, ELS aims to subsidize the reduction of transaction costs by providing a "zero width" market that in effect serves to capture a micro-spread while also reducing adverse selection bias. In general, the risk reducing leg of ELS execution is discriminatory and will not trade against market momentum.

Complement to Traditional Execution Services

ELS differs from traditional services employed by electronic trading desks in that it focuses on the short-term elimination of adverse selection, and it seeks to achieve neutral to positive short-term returns (e.g. capture zero or positive spread). ELS is complementary to longer term electronic trading strategies that employ order slicing. For example, if order slicing methods permit discretion across a time window, ELS can execute parent orders within the window in an efficient manner using signal-based methods.

ELS aims to enhance access to liquidity sources that are often not accessible due to the competitive advantages short-term liquidity providers have over institutional traders. Furthermore, ELS does not aim to reduce access to the liquidity provided by short-term liquidity providers *per se*, but seeks to change the fundamental economics of its interactions with short-term liquidity providers.

Measuring Execution Performance

Because of the difference in the notional size and time horizons of the two investment strategies, the concepts utilized within TCA to measure market impact of institutional orders are often at odds with "mark up" metrics traditionally utilized by short-term liquidity providers. Market making (short-term) approaches are often concerned with improving bookable edge, where the market has not moved against the market maker position (i.e. where the short-term trade result is not a loss). In this context, metrics that institutions often associate with short-term market impact might also correspond to conditions favorable to "active" market making strategies which aim to recycle inventory in a manner that captures an effective spread whilst positioning for the right side of market momentum. Conversely, traditional TCA of institutional orders has focused on implementation shortfall vs. arrival price, measuring the slippage incurred when the average execution price is traded at a premium compared to the original arrival price. Traditional methodologies employed in TCA, such as implementation shortfall, utilize averaged price information on institutional orders. This technique unfortunately ignores the individual fills and exogenous trade and quote price movements that occur before and after each of the fills that comprise an institutional order.

The key to rationalizing the two concepts is in measuring *market impact* independent of *positive alpha* (i.e. "edge capture"), and true *price improvement* independent of *negative alpha* (i.e. "adverse fills"). By examining each fill in the context of the NBBO quote at which it traded as well as all previous fills executed for an order, the implementation shortfall can be decomposed such that the market impact of the institutional order can be isolated from effective liquidity sourcing, and the actual price improvement provided by effective liquidity provision strategies can be separated from adverse selection. In light of recent developments in alpha-adjusted post-trade analysis,[37] a number of promising TCA

---

[37] Borkovec, M., Tuttle, L., Tyurin K., Zhao, Z. "Alpha- Optimized Trading Schedules: Identifying Own Price Impact in Realized Returns." 2011.

decomposition techniques offer a potential measurement solution for institutional desks wishing to focus on both the macro strategy (e.g. time, volume and signal-based slicing) and the micro strategy (effective liquidity sourcing) of their electronic execution channels, and also serve to bridge the gap between performance metrics used by institutional trading desks and short-term liquidity providers.

Conclusion

This paper defines Electronic Liquidity Strategy (ELS), a new approach that aims to level the playing field between institutional investors that need to source liquidity and short-term liquidity providers that operate in an opportunistic and discriminatory manner. ELS seeks to capture a micro-spread, achieve favorable economics from market fee structure, avoid adverse selection, and improve access to available liquidity across a fragmented marketplace. In many cases ELS seeks to benefit from key competitive advantages commonly utilized by short-term liquidity providers by employing techniques such as microstructure-based execution signals, low latency order placement, sophisticated special order types, order flow discrimination and advantages provided by exchange membership status. ELS can be implemented in a manner that is complementary to traditional execution services that employ order slicing methods. ELS is a necessary evolution of electronic trading services in the highly competitive US equity electronic marketplace that has overly catered to high frequency traders and internalizers that benefit from exchange and market structure advantages – advantages that ELS aims to utilize for the benefit of institutional traders.

http://www.itg.com/news_events/papers/Alpha_Algo.pdf

VI. Reforming the National Market System

Haim Bodek
Decimus Capital Markets, LLC / Haim Bodek ConsultingSM
January 2013

Introduction

When the Tabb Group released its US Equity Market Structure Confidence Survey Result in August 2012, few were surprised that it concluded that institutional investor confidence in US equities market structure was perhaps the worst it had ever been. Equity outflows had been recorded for the 16 consecutive months, market volumes were off 50% from their peak, and almost 50% of institutional investors surveyed wanted regulators to step in.

The problem of market fragmentation was cited as a primary concern, a notion intimately connected to the unprecedented complexity of the US marketplace. By August 2012, the stock market had become what I refer to as the *arena* – a highly competitive network of 13 stock exchanges and approximately 50 alternative trading facilities and dark pools. Regulation NMS, the regulatory framework meant to bind these venues into a coherent national market system, had been introduced a mere five years before in 2007. And clearly, the *arena* has stressed the Regulation NMS framework well beyond its anticipated scope.

Furthermore, a new type of market participant had emerged into the fray – the high frequency trader. HFTs, as they were called, the gladiators of the new electronic marketplace, had stepped confidently into the *arena* and they had prevailed. Christening themselves as the "new market makers," they dominated the electronic marketplace with opaque trading strategies that accounted for an astonishing estimated 50%-70% of US equities volume. These masters of the highly fragmented electronic marketplace attributed their success to expert abilities in exploiting speed, plumbing, and obscure tactics in the market microstructure. And yet, this claim was only in part the truth.

HFTs weren't the "quant" savants they claimed, but were in fact masters of "regulatory arbitrage." Their unusual rise to dominance had coincided near simultaneously with the introduction of Regulation NMS in 2007, rules which were meant provide a fair and non-discriminatory marketplace for long-term investors. Modern HFT strategies thrived in the new electronic marketplace, seemingly tuned perfectly to the implementations of Regulation NMS that precisely dictated the inner working of the marketplace, including price movement and order handling. By circumventing the intent of Regulation NMS with a myriad of legal exceptions and clever regulatory workarounds, HFTs exploited fragmentation to their benefit at the expense of institutional investors.

Indeed, the ugly truth was that electronic exchanges had aggressively courted HFTs and had in the process sold out the institutional investor. Under the pretense of innovation, for-profit exchanges had catered to HFT firms, accommodating their strategies with specialized order types that advantaged them over other investors. Many exchange features introduced as innovations were in fact features designed to assist HFTs in "regulatory arbitrage" activities that circumvented Regulation NMS to get an edge over other traders in the marketplace.

By August 2012, the Flash Crash, the BATS Crash, the Faceplant, the Knightmare, all had taken their toll on investor confidence. However the daily grind was even more discouraging as institutional investors tried to navigate a murky market structure, forced to play a high-stakes game where every card appeared to be stacked against them. For the institutional investor, plagued by mini-flash crashes, phantom prices, and rapid withdrawal of liquidity, there was little reason for confidence in the new marketplace, which had become simply unmanageable and unrecognizable.

The Tabb Group was just confirming what we knew all along, that US equity markets have a chronic disease. I assert that the disease is in fact modern HFT, and more precisely HFT exploitation of Regulation NMS to the detriment of the investing public, ironically the definitive body of regulation meant to protect long-term investors. At the September 20th Senate hearing on high frequency trading, Senators Reed and Crapo were provided testimony that HFT had produced a "casino-like environment" and that the situation has reached a "crisis point." NYSE CEO Duncan Niederauer publicly stated that "nobody rational would look at this [market] and say it isn't broken." And we find ourselves now at crossroads on how to address what has indeed become a market structure crisis in the US equities marketplace.

For a decade, HFTs and exchanges had worked together to assert influence over the market structure itself, tilting the balance in favor of the "new market makers." In the pursuit of an electronic marketplace that served their interests, they betrayed the long-term investor and sacrificed the integrity of the national market system itself. The situation has reached a crisis point, and it is now time to reassess and take corrective action. It is time to truly level the playing field.

Indeed, I am vigorously optimistic about our prospects for strengthening the US equities marketplace. I assert that there is a straightforward path to correcting the system. The industry took a wrong turn when Regulation NMS was implemented market-wide in 2007. To address the market structure crisis head on, we need to reassess Regulation NMS in the context of its original purpose and intent – to bind a fragmented marketplace into an effective national market system that serves long term investors.

Thus I argue that Regulation NMS needs to be upgraded to be more resilient and to provide truly fair and non-discriminatory access for long-term investors to what has become a highly fragmented US equities marketplace. In particular, the specific implementation of the Market Access Rule and the Order Protection Rule, both mandated by Regulation NMS, needs to be substantially reviewed and made robust against circumvention by regulatory arbitrageurs. We also need to eliminate features of the market structure that have served special interests at the expense of the interest of the greater marketplace itself.

And now, without further ado, here is the proposed 10 step plan:

A 10 Step Proposal for Reforming the National Market System

1. Eliminate unfair and discriminatory HFT advantages

Exchanges need to eliminate unfair and discriminatory advantages that cater to high frequency traders, especially with regard to special order types and order matching engine features that accommodate HFT strategies. To the extent that lines were crossed from grey into black with regard to the principles-based laws of the Exchange Act of 1934, the offending parties must be held accountable.

2. Strengthen the Market Access Rule of Reg NMS

Rule 610, the Market Access Rule, dictates how the prices from a fragmented marketplace are bound into a unified national best bid and offer. It also constrains the permissible mechanics of how price moves occur and how customer orders are handled, as well as banning locked markets where the buy price and sell price are equal across multiple venues. If we are to address the problem of HFT in the US markets, we have to carefully reassess and strengthen the Market Access Rule to protect the integrity of the marketplace, which means reassessing and solving the problem of locked markets in a manner that serves long term investors. More specifically, a full or partial repeal of the ban on locked markets should be considered as suggested by Senator Ted Kaufman in his Aug 5, 2010 letter to the SEC.

3. Limit exceptions to the Order Protection Rule of Reg NMS

Rule 611, the Order Protection Rule, is intended to protect against trade-throughs, where trades occur at inferior prices to what should be available at the national best bid and offer. However, this rule provides an exception which permits a firm to trade though the national best bid or offer using special order types. While this exception was meant for institutions that needed to sweep the book to obtain instantaneous access to liquidity at multiple price points, the exception has been undermined by HFTs who exploit it with special order types that trade ahead investors whose orders are held back by slower price feeds. Rule 611 needs to be constrained so that it cannot be abused by HFT participants or used in conjunction with direct price feeds to unfairly step ahead of public customers.

4. Expose off-exchange trades to greater competition

We need to shift more of the retail order flow that is internalized off-exchange back onto the traditional lit exchanges. Exchanges will be able to diversify their customer bases away from high frequency traders when a healthy diversity of order flow is routed to them. One straightforward and proven solution would be to require trades that are negotiated off-exchange to be exposed to the electronic crowd on-exchange for competitive price improvement, a practice which benefits retail customers and enhances the liquidity made available to the public marketplace.

5. Address excessive cancellation rates and fleeting liquidity

Regulators need to address the explosion of data that is a result of a market microstructure environment that caters to high frequency traders. We are at the point where it is necessary to create a US equities message traffic plan to throttle rapidly canceled orders that have no economic benefit and are disruptive and burdensome to the greater marketplace. A minimum order resting time of 10ms would go a long way in limiting the negative impact of HFT "spam and cancel" strategies that currently thrive in US equity markets. Another solution would be to impose SEC-mandated fees for excessive cancellation rates.

6. Re-invigorate market maker incentives

To the degree that advantages and asymmetries exist in the market for certain classes of participants, such advantages must be made completely transparent and for the most part should be associated with adequate performance in meeting market maker obligations. The movement away from official market maker roles at many venues has resulted in an overall market environment where the "new market makers" (i.e. HFTs) share no responsibility in serving the investing public, maintaining fair and orderly markets, or developing concentrated order flow sources into the venue. The re-establishment of market making roles with incentives will assist in enhancing the integrity and liquidity of the marketplace.

7. Mandate comprehensive disclosures on execution quality

Buy side clients do not have adequate transparency into the order handling and execution performance of ECNs, dark pools, internalizers, and smart order routers. Not only do these entities need to be subjected to a higher level of regulatory oversight and disclosure, they need to provide clients more comprehensive information so that clients can fulfill their fiduciary obligations with regard to best execution requirements in a highly fragmented marketplace. Such disclosures should be mandated by regulators and should be robust enough for buy side clients to identify common abuses such as "trading ahead" and "latency arbitrage."

8. Reassess US equity market fee structure

Currently, the major stock exchanges reward the highest volume participants with a superior fee structure. One impact is to give an anti-competitive advantage to the largest HFTs, who may in fact also be benefitting as exchange owners, a situation which subsidizes the largest participants at the expense of smaller participants who pay higher fees and receive lower rebates. The net impact is to limit diversity and to penalize smaller liquidity providers. Overall, the usage of fee structure to penalize certain customers and reward others should be constrained if not eliminated altogether. In addition, there is a currently a fee cap of $0.0030 for taker fees, which provides an upper bound on the rebate kickbacks that drive the profits of HFTs. Given the dominance of the maker-taker model, a reduction in the fee cap should be considered to encourage the development of more robust volumes on exchanges that run alternative market models.

9. Enhance market quality with appropriate price increments and size constraints

Decimalization was by far a net positive for US equities markets. However, the impact on liquidity was unbalanced across names, and there is room for improvement by fine-tuning price increments and managing odd lot trade frequency. Clearly, investors would be served by permitting sub-penny price improvement (which could be invisible) in low-price names such as BAC. The depth of posted liquidity in high priced names such as AAPL would be encouraged by wider price increments. There are also strong arguments for tuning tick increments for names differently depending on market capitalization to provide a better value proposition for market makers in less liquid names. The excessive use of small size odd lots by HFT pinging strategies for predatory purposes could be constrained by requiring minimum sizes or by constraining the frequency of small size orders.

10. Eliminate the self-regulatory status of for-profit exchanges

The notion of for-profit exchanges maintaining their status as self-regulatory organizations (SROs) must be challenged. The ongoing potential for the business development activities of such exchanges to interfere with their self-regulatory obligations is a very real systemic risk to the marketplace. At the bare minimum, for-profit exchanges must be frequently scrutinized by regulators to ensure that their business development interests are not compromising their ability to maintain fair and non-discriminatory markets.

Conclusion

The market structure debate is complex, but one thing is clear to the majority of insiders – we need to restore investor confidence in the US equities marketplace. And this means we need to further evolve US equities markets to achieve the purpose and intent of Regulation NMS. The work will not be complete until we create a national market system that effectively binds a fragmented marketplace into a cohesive system, one that truly serves the needs of long-term investors, and that provides comprehensive liquidity for capital formation and long-term growth.

There is a growing community within the financial establishment of core insiders who support a comprehensive overhaul of US equities market structure along many of the lines I have described. If we make progress on only a fraction of the points I have described, I am optimistic that we will see market structure shift to service the needs of the long-term investor. If we make progress on all points, the US marketplace will have restored its status as a national market system without rival among the capital markets.

VII. Haim Bodek Interview with NZZ

Interview with the Swiss newspaper Neue Zürcher Zeitung
Haim Bodek interviewed by Christof Leisinger
Decimus Capital Markets, LLC / Haim Bodek Consulting SM
November 2012

Interview published December 2012
<u>**"Investors are paying the price for fragmented markets"**</u>
Christof Leisinger, Neue Zürcher Zeitung

CL: *Credit Suisse seeks reportedly the US regulatory nod to run an exchange. What are your thoughts about this plan?*

HB: From what I understand, the proposed exchange in question, Light Pool, is an investor friendly exchange that is designed to protect against predatory high frequency trading activity on its venue. Frankly, I am sympathetic to Credit Suisse taking a step in the right direction to create an investor-centric market model. By seeking exchange status, Light Pool will be better positioned to compete against exchanges that have catered to high frequency traders at the expense of institutional investors.

CL: *Are you concerned about potential conflicts of interest that could arise from an exchange owned outright by one of the big investment banks?*

HB: I am much more concerned about HFT ownership and influence on the exchanges, which in my opinion have contributed significantly to the current market structure crisis. Banks currently run dark pools and internalization desks -- entities that are much less transparent and which are not required to meet the high regulatory standards imposed on exchanges. Hence what Credit Suisse is proposing with

Light Pool is a positive step toward more regulatory oversight and transparency. While conflicts of interest are a serious concern, I am of the opinion that investment banks are much more experienced in managing such complexities when compared to other types of exchange owners. I'd rather see a top-tier investment bank take leadership on cultivating a new exchange, than see additional exchanges set up by HFT insiders that are more experienced at taking advantage of institutional investors than serving them.

CL: *What is the incentive to run an exchange at all? Is there a lot of money to be made?*

HB: The margins in the exchange space will continue to compress. Excessive fragmentation and competition have made it difficult to differentiate the value proposition of any single venue. It is a tougher business than ever. What is really at stake now is liquidity. Investment banks that have built significant equities franchises must not only provide a superior and comprehensive product offering, but they must demonstrate the ability to attract dense concentrations of liquidity from natural buyers and sellers. In these market conditions, any investment in the exchange space is better understood when taking into account the strategic position of the investor's franchise and the potential impact on related business units. Liquidity is and will continue to be the key differentiator for quite some time.

CL: *How, why and who is paying the price?*

HB: At this point, and despite conflicting academic research and debate that often seems thoroughly misinformed about the inner workings of US equity markets, institutional investors are well aware that they are indeed the ones paying the price. Especially in the last five years, predatory high frequency trading and excessive fragmentation have increased effective execution costs. The significant infrastructure and technology expenses that are required to adequately access US equities market venues are indirectly passed to investors. The cost to institutional investors of execution slippages, rapidly diminishing and/or phantom liquidity, and the frequent market disruptions associated with predatory high frequency trading is difficult to estimate across the industry, but is obviously attributable in part to the unusual and lucrative profitability of HFT firms over the last five years.

CL: *Alternative mechanisms and locations for trading securities are mushrooming. Does this make sense?*

HB: The mushrooming of trading venues is both a cause and symptom of the current market structure crisis. Excessive fragmentation has reduced the effectiveness of the marketplace, and these new venues aim to provide a solution. There may be merits in many new business models, but I fear that the cumulative cost of excessive fragmentation in US equities markets has become an overall net negative to the investing public.

CL: *Is it in the interest of investors in their search for minimizing the costs of finding a counterparty?*

HB: Institutional investors are not doing enough to assert influence over the fragmentation issue by voting with their volume. They have outsourced their problems to sell-side brokers, many of which run dark pools which are direct competitors to exchanges. More often than not, the dark pools are as toxic as the lit exchanges, and they are trading with the same counterparties in even less transparent environments. I would argue institutional investors would be better served by engaging their brokers to make better use of the traditional exchanges. Furthermore, exchanges need to do more to serve the needs of institutional investors and to wean themselves off HFT customer volume.

CL: *Which role do algorithmic trading ventures play in this game? ... and especially the so called High-Frequency-Traders? They are said to have advantages over normal investors. How is it possible and how does it come?*

HB: HFTs are very sophisticated market participants. Sell-side brokers of the major investment banks pale in comparison. The issue with HFT firms is that they are highly discriminatory, always demanding an edge to trade. If they don't find that edge on a venue, they will move on to another market. In the mid-2000s, the collapse of the specialist model and the rise of dark pools made exchanges highly dependent on HFT order flow. The vigorous competition between exchanges for HFT order flow resulted in the introduction of a number of specialized order types and order matching engines features which served to accommodate HFT strategies. Many of these features were introduced under the pretense of innovation, but in practice served to advantage those HFT firms who worked closely with exchanges to tune the feature sets to their specific needs. The frequency of these HFT-oriented exchange innovations intensified after Regulation NMS was introduced in 2007. One can argue the merits and reasons for each specific exchange modification, but it is hard to dismiss the fact that US equities market structure is heavily tilted toward accommodating the activity of high frequency traders. For the record, I do agree that sell-side brokers need to do more to leverage the features typically employed by high frequency traders, including advanced order types, in servicing the needs of their clients. However, it is also clear to me that exchanges need to be forthright about how functionality is used by high frequency traders to gain an advantage over other market participants.

CL: *Are you surprised that many investors lost their confidence in the integrity of the markets after different flash-crashes as well as the BATS-debacle and the "Knightmare"?*

HB: The current state of US equities market structure has alienated very sophisticated investors -- and I count myself in that category. It appears that the main market participants who defend the status quo in the US equities markets are the ones who have benefitted disproportionately from deep asymmetries in the market over the last five years. I am encouraged that NYSE CEO Duncan Niederauer has gone on the record saying that "nobody rational would look at this [market] and say it isn't broken." Larry Tabb, a world-class leading expert on market structure, echoed similar concerns at the recent Senate hearing on HFT and market structure organized by Senators Reed and Crapo. We are really at crossroads on how to address what has become a market structure crisis in the US equities marketplace.

CL: *What has to change to restore it?*

HB: There is actually a reasonable way forward to correcting the system -- the industry took a wrong turn when Regulation NMS was implemented market-wide in 2007. We need to reassess Regulation NMS in the context of its original purpose and intent to bind a fragmented marketplace into an effective national market system that serves long term investors. However, it will take some will-power from the industry to openly discuss the core issues, which means some parties would implicitly admit a degree of culpability in either benefiting or being disadvantaged by the current system.

First, exchanges need to eliminate unfair and discriminatory advantages that cater to high frequency traders. To the extent that lines were crossed from grey into black with regard to the principles-based laws of the

Exchange Act of 1934, the offending parties must be held accountable.

Second, Regulation NMS needs to be upgraded to be more resilient to provide truly fair and non-discriminatory access for long-term investors to what has become a highly fragmented US equities marketplace In particular, the specific implementation of Market Access Rule and Order Protection Rule needs to be substantially reviewed and made robust against circumvention by regulatory arbitrageurs.

Third, the notion for-profit exchanges maintaining their status as self-regulatory organizations (SROs) needs to be challenged. Speaking from experience, the ongoing potential for the business development activities of exchanges to interfere with their self-regulatory obligations is a very real systemic risk to the marketplace.

Fourth, we need to shift more of the order flow that is internalized off-exchange back onto the traditional "lit" exchanges. Exchanges will be able to diversify their customer bases away from high frequency traders when a healthy diversity of order flow is routed to them. For one, I'd like to see internalized trades in equities subjected to competition from the electronic crowd on exchange, a practice which has proven itself in the US equity options markets where it is mandated by regulations. Furthermore, ECNs, dark pools, and order routing practices need to be subjected to a higher level of regulatory oversight and disclosure. The US equities marketplace as a whole is way too opaque as it currently stands.

CL: *Are you optimistic that it will happen?*

HB: Yes, I am optimistic that we will see market structure shift to service the needs of the long-term investor. There is a growing community of core insiders that support an overhaul of US equities market structure along the lines I have described. One issue with traction is that there are many fiduciary issues at stake, and my sense is that liability concerns are holding up the reform process and open dialogue. Regardless, it is pretty clear that the market structure issue in the US isn't going away until something is done.

CL: *Do we need a switch back to centralized non-for profit-exchanges having all orders routed to [a single market center]?*

HB: No, we don't need to go backward. We need to further evolve US equities markets to achieve the purpose and intent of Regulation NMS, which is the creation of a national market system that binds a fragmented marketplace into a cohesive system that truly serves the needs of long-term investors, providing comprehensive liquidity for capital formation and long-term growth.

VIII. Haim Bodek Interview with TradeTech

Interview with the TradeTech
Haim Bodek interviewed by Kelly Hushin
Decimus Capital Markets, LLC / Haim Bodek Consulting ᔕᴹ
November 2012

Interviewed Conducted for TradeTech USA 2013
Topic: HFT - An Artificial Industry
Speaker: Haim Bodek
Link: TradeTech, Feb 26-28, 2013, New York

KH: *What was it was like to work with Scott Patterson on his book, Dark Pools? What was the catalyst was to tell your story through that outlet?*

HB: He caught me at a sensitive, delicate time. I was angry about a number of deep market structure features. There was a particular algorithmic trading tradition that I bumped my head up against. I felt I needed to correct it or defeat it in some way. I was introduced to him by one of his other sources, who felt that I could illuminate some of the aspects of the HFT industry that were not generally talked about in the greater news and the community.

I worked with Scott to educate him about scalping practices and how special order types work and how exchange order matching engine features benefit HFT. I showed him how opaque and non-transparent many of those features were, and how, in many ways, the industry had taken advantage of the buy side and institutions to benefit certain types of firms running specific strategies.

KH: *How might orders that "Hide and Light" provide an advantage for high-speed traders?*

80

HB: Orders that hide and light are a clever work around the ban on locked markets, which is a regulation NMS rule; a constraint that prohibited firms from locking the market. There are hide not slide orders, post no preference blind, price to comply, BATS only...these orders permit certain firms that are usually quite sophisticated, to lock a market for a brief amount of time (that's when these orders are in a hidden state), and then when the market moves, these orders can light up.

Now, in themselves, if they're designed correctly, and documented correctly, and used by the majority of participants in the right way, they might not be so bad. The problem is there are quite a number of perks that were thrown in that serve to advantage certain types of traders, thrown in as perks with these orders – and these features are actually one of the main reasons I became a market structure reform advocate.

One of those features was reported in the Wall Street Journal. It's called "queue jumping," and allows a hide not slide order to get ahead of other orders in a way that, I would argue, is a violation of price-time priority order precedence rules at the exchanges.

KH: *At your previous firm, Trading Machines, you leveraged high-speed trading technologies, and for a brief period, orders that hide and light. You spoke about how you started to become a bit more of an advocate for transparency, but why did you, as a high frequency trader, want to engage the SEC to bring transparency to the issues around these special orders? What was your goal there?*

HB: I came to the conclusion that if you weren't playing the HFT game, while you could improve your execution performance quite considerably by using some of the techniques and order types, really the entire ecosystem itself had been distorted. There was really a situation where you either had to join them and become a stock trader – a high frequency trader just focused on the stock market. I was more on the option side of business.

I felt that the stock market had basically become so distorted that it was negatively impacting other algorithmic trading traditions and really destroying the diversity that should exist in the market.

KH: *My next question is about exchange officials who have said that their order types and work is fully disclosed. Would you agree with that statement?*

HB: A good example would be queue jumping which is a feature that is often marketed directly to firms, to high frequency traders primarily, which is not in any way supported by exchange documentation. There are a number of other perks, many of which are not disclosed yet or documented in any capacity. I came to the conclusion that a smart person could figure things out if they had access to the documentation. A lot of features people think are documented... but if you actually go and look for the documentation, you'll find they aren't. So how do people learn about it? They learn about it from other people in the industry. It's a little bit of a closed club that really has to be broken for the markets to move on.

KH: *What advice would you have for the buy side traders who are operating in markets where high-speed traders might have an edge? What can they do? What would you tell them?*

HB: The first step is to realize that the features and the order types used by HFT – these exchanges have become so dominated by HFT-oriented activity that if you aren't using those features and those order types in the correct way, you're really on the wrong side of the slippage of equation.

It's not about picking up the rebate. It's about getting really fair and neutral access to the exchange and if you're not using an HFT-oriented exchange correctly, you're probably falling into many of the abuses that I experienced prior to learning about how these features work.

You have to learn how to use the exchange correctly. Until regulators step in and change the microstructure, it's really an obligation on the sell side brokers and the buy side to operate and access the markets more like an HFT would. I'm not really trying to advocate for HFT. I'm really advocating for transparency and documentation on these features and then a general knowledge across industry that these features matter. Getting to the top of the queue matters.

If you don't use the mechanisms to compete correctly, you're going to be at the back of the queue and that's disadvantaging you or your client.

KH: *You speak at quite a lot of industry events. You're going to speak at TradeTech. Why is it important to talk about this with the industry or to be in front of people spreading the word?*

I felt, at one point, that either there'd be significant backlash and I'd have to defend myself against these allegations. That was my original concern. But what's happened more recently is that the feedback is, "You're right about these details!" But people don't want to talk about them and we're in a situation where we either need to eliminate features from the market or we need everybody to know about them and can operate correctly. I'm doing that now because I'm one of the primary individuals that kicked this off. I'd say there are other people who are very happy with the work that I'm doing and I'd like to see them out there educating.

KH: *How long do you think it will take for the industry to band together and get ahold of this issue?*

HB: I think that the first step is, literally, the major sell side investment banks need to do a deep dive and understand how HFT is operated. I mean it came out of nowhere and they have a huge amount of catch up to do. They're probably five or six years behind the HFT crowd. I think it's going to be difficult to have a really meaningful dialogue until the banks do the real work to learn about a comprehensive feature set. I'm trying to point people in right direction with some of the articles I am doing on TABB Forum.

On the other hand, as I said, I think the exchanges have not been transparent. I think that they have treated different customer bases quite differently. I think they're going to need to come clean and come forth and treat customers with the same level of information, provision and transparency. We're not seeing that either yet. So it's a little bit of a matchmaking situation right now. We need the banks to really lean on the exchanges and that's starting now. In the last six weeks, there's definitely been a lot of activity with regard to the topic I just described, but we're just at the beginning of it.

KH: *As someone who's seen both sides of the HFT industry and understands HFT in and out – an argument I hear a lot is that it's "just faster." Do you think that argument will continue to hold up, or have we all realized there's more to it than that?*

HB: I fell for that argument. If you're using the wrong order types and executing in the wrong way, you're going to have my experience. I got faster and faster and faster and I was just the first guy to fall into the trap. It got ridiculous, to the point where I thought I had a bug. That's what the story in Dark Pools was.

The story of HFT is really that the microstructure features are where the key advantage was. It wasn't speed. Speed was necessary to extract the value of those features. The way I think of it is, you walk into your house, you open the front door, and someone's standing in the foyer. You say, "How did you get there?" and he says, "I was really fast I ran by you." No. Actually, you took the back door.

That's what we're trying to do here is to enforce across industry a transparency, so that these back doors either are known to everyone or they are eliminated. As I said, queue jumping was one of them that is extremely important to HFT profitability and it was not generally known about until, you know, six to eight weeks ago.

Appendix A: Resources on Stock Market Reform

Books

Patterson, S. "Dark Pools." New York: Random House, Inc., 2012.

"To that end, in the summer of 2011, [Bodek] decided to explain it all to federal regulators. He hired a major law firm to help him use his understanding of toxic order types he'd gained from his exchange contacts while at Trading Machines, combined with the detail of his understanding of high-frequency strategies he'd learned from the 0+ Scalping Strategy document, to lay out a road map. The road map detailed his argument that high-speed traders and exchanges had created an unfair market that was hurting nearly all investors."

Dark Pools details the rise of electronic trading in the US stock market over the last two decades. It also dedicates a number of chapters to my personal odyssey to alert regulators to the unfair and discriminatory features provided by electronic exchanges that serve to advantage HFTs over the public customer.

Arnuk, S. and Saluzzi, J. "Broken Markets." FT Press, 2012.

"The changes brought about by Reg NMS have turned the market from an investor-focused mechanism, which welcomes investors of all types and speeds, to a sub second, trader-focused mechanism, where the concerns and confidence of investors are an afterthought."

Sal Arnuk and Joe and Saluzzi have been at the forefront of the market structure reform debate from the very start and their book is required reading. Senator Ted Kaufman wrote the forward. You should also read their blog at http://themistrading.com.

Connaughton, J. "The Payoff." Prospecta Press, 2012.

"Ted must have been thinking the same thing. Near the end of the meeting he told Schapiro, "I don't believe you're going to do anything about high-frequency trading." Looking him straight in the eye, she replied, "You just watch." We watched for nearly three years. It wasn't until July 2011 and June 2012 that the SEC approved minimalist rules that would force market participants to collect the data that would enable the SEC to begin—begin—the process of understanding HFT's impact on markets. In effect, Ted and I and America are still watching and waiting for the SEC to take meaningful action."

Jeff Connaughton worked alongside Senator Ted Kaufman as they tried to implement realistic financial reforms in the wake of the financial crisis. Connaughton exposes the difficulties of addressing financial reform in a system ripe with conflicts of interest. The chapter on their work to address HFT is eye-opening to say the least.

News, Articles, and Commentary

"Tradeworx, Inc. Public Commentary on SEC Market Structure Concept Release" - Manoj Narang, Tradeworx Inc., April 2010

"Jumping ahead of an order that was placed earlier at the same price by another trader is an UNFAIR practice, because it undermines the principle of PRICE-TIME priority on which our equity markets are premised. Unfortunately, this UNFAIR practice is widespread, due to a deficiency in Rule 611 of Regulation NMS. HFTs should not be blamed for exploiting it – in fact, many HFTs who exploit this deficiency do so unwittingly."

In 2010, Manoj Narang submitted to the SEC this overview of the universe of HFT trading strategies and his concerns with regard to market structure reform. Most notable is his validation of price-time priority corruption within the implementation of REG NMS framework at electronic exchanges. This submission clearly presents evidence of what I consider the tip of the iceberg of microstructure asymmetries that serve to advantage HFTs over the public customer.

"8/5/10 letter to the SEC" – Senator Ted Kaufman, August 2010

"Some commentators have suggested that the SEC should lift the ban on locked markets. ... ...in the current high-speed, highly-fragmented marketplace, banning locked markets might have several unintended consequences, including slowing down trading and creating uncertainty regarding market prices. ... Accordingly, the current prohibition on locked markets can slow down trading in ways that may disadvantage long-term investors."

Kaufman's nine point plan sets the standard for a realistic path to correct deep market structure problems with US equity markets. I contend that Kaufman's letter still serves as the best framework yet put forward, and should be used as a starting point for reigniting the debate on US stock market reform.

"Is the NBBO being Ignored?" - Eric Hunsader, Nanex, LLC, July 2011

"Per Reg NMS, the NBBO for a stock is defined to mean the best bid/offer sent by a market center to the Security Information Processor known as the SIP (CQS, UQDF). But *no one* uses the SIP for that anymore, we are often told, which would seem to violate the letter and spirit of Reg NMS. We'd like to note that last year, 2.5 million subscribers spent over $450 million to receive and process CQS."

Eric Hunsader has been at the forefront of the HFT debate from the very start. The research unit of his firm specializes in tick data analysis. Many of the data extracts Nanex provides to the market at no charge are well beyond the capabilities of most major investment banks. Eric's work on exchanges failing to properly honor the SIP feed is of particular interest, especially in light of the recent SEC action against NYSE for allowing impermissible delays in SIP feeds while providing low-latency price feeds products to sophisticated customers. Be sure to check out the full Nanex website which can be found at http://www.nanex.net/.

"For Superfast Stock Traders, a Way to Jump Ahead in Line" - Scott Patterson & Jenny Strasburg, WSJ, 9/19/12

"Haim Bodek was a Wall Street insider at Goldman Sachs and UBS before launching his own trading firm. Now he is taking on the financial establishment that spawned him."

This is the first article that explicitly described the queue jumping special order type abuse and my role in alerting regulators to these practices.

"Written Testimony to the United States Senate Committee on Banking, Housing, and Urban Affairs Washington, DC September 20, 2012" - Larry Tabb, Tabb Group, September 2012

"Currently, most exchanges post their order types; however, the descriptions of what they do and how they work are not tremendously intuitive. Exchanges, and for that matter ATSs, ECNs, internalizers and even brokers need to begin to provide greater transparency, descriptions, and concrete examples of how each order type works, how fees/rebates are generated, where they show up in the book queue, how and when they route out, and how these order types change under the various market conditions. If these entities are not willing to be more transparent, then maybe that is one way to limit the number of matching licenses."

One day after the front-page WSJ article came out which detailed my concerns with special order types, a Senate hearing was held on market structure where Larry Tabb made the statement above in reference to advantages embedded in HFT-oriented order types. I was thrilled that a person of his stature was finally addressing an issue that the industry had been treating with kid gloves since the first news about HFT advantages came out about it a full eight months earlier in February 2012.[38]

"Analysis: Complaints rise over complex U.S. stock orders" - Herbert Lash, Reuters, 10/19/12

"Allegations of abuse over how a stock trade is executed may soon bring a new black eye to Wall Street or amount to little more than another warning about high-frequency trading…"

This article covers many different viewpoints on the controversy surrounding HFT-oriented order types and the close relationship between exchanges and HFTs. Some of

---

[38] Mehta, N. and Gallu, J.. "SEC Reviewing U.S. Trading Practices After Decade-Long Shift to Automation"
Bloomberg News, 25, Feb 25, 2012
http://www.businessweek.com/news/2012-02-25/sec-reviewing-u-dot-s-dot-trading-practices-after-decade-long-shift-to-automation

the statements made by sources I found discouraging, but the expansion of the order type probe in November proved that it is still too early to draw conclusions on how regulators will act.

"The Complexity of High Frequency Trading" – Jaffray Woodriff, QIM, November 2012

"The SEC and CFTC, led by Congress, should undertake a holistic effort to reduce undue complexity in our regulatory system. This effort would fit well within your regulatory "pay go" proposals and would be akin to the Paperwork Reduction Act of 1995. The government should aspire to make the equities market meet the simplicity and transparency of the futures market."

Jaffray Woodriff, of Quantitative Investment Management, wrote this concise review of the current state of the market structure reform debate, arguing for a reform of cash equities markets using the simplicity of US futures markets as the appropriate market model. Check out his blog at http://transparentsimplicity.com.

"Exchanges Get Close Inspection" - Scott Patterson & Jean Eaglesham, WSJ, 11/19/12

"The order-type probe was a "come to Jesus moment" for regulators about how exchanges appear to have systematically developed trading advantages for certain sophisticated clients, often with insufficient regulatory oversight or understanding of products."

This article details the expansion of the special order type probe by the Office of Compliance, Inspections, and Examinations of the SEC, which is a very significant development. The quote above gives some insight into how the topic of HFT advantages embedded in special order types is viewed (as reported by an insider source).

<u>"Exchanges Fault Complexity"</u>– Scott Patterson, WSJ, 12/17/12

"Joe Mecane, head of U.S. equities at NYSE Euronext, told the committee that some of the exchange operator's order types were designed to comply with regulations, while others were written to 'guarantee economic results' for clients."

At the December Senate hearing on market structure, the advantages embedded in special order types were discussed even more extensively than in the September hearing. I have a great deal of respect for the leadership Joe Mecane displayed at the hearing, which was similar to Larry Tabb's honest testimony at the September Senate hearing. Believe me, it isn't easy for an exchange executive to go on the record to argue for such changes.

Appendix B: HFT Scalping Example

The following example illustrates the economics of a potential sequence for a simple HFT scalping trade with an impending sweep event. Note that this example implicitly assumes that the HFT has access to the appropriate fee structure (e.g. most favorable exchange volume tiers, superior clearing rates).

1. Initial conditions:
    1.1. NBBO 30.00 X 30.01
    1.2. Exchange A 30.00 bid for 1000; Exchange B 30.00 bid for 1000
    1.3. HFT resting order at top-of-queue top-of-book 30.00 bid for 100 on Exchange A. One method of achieving this superior queue position is through special order types combined with spamming. Note that such spamming is designed to achieve queue position, not to impact the network or spoof pricing.

	$29.98	$29.99	$30.00 Inside	$30.01	$30.02	$30.03
NBBO			2,000 shares	2,000 shares		
Exchange A	1,000 shares	1,000 shares	100 shares HFT / 900 shares institutional	1,000 shares	1,000 shares	500 shares
Exchange B	500 shares	500 shares	1,000 shares	1,000 shares	500 shares	500 shares

HFT Buy top-of-queue top-of-book

2. Incoming sell 1000 at 30.00 order on Exchange A hits bid, clearing Exchange A's book @ 30.00; HFT resting 30.00 bid for 100 is taken out. HFT collects rebate on this first leg of the trade.

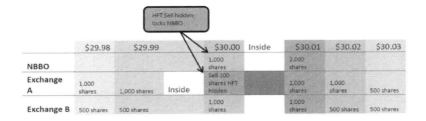

	$29.98	$29.99	$30.00	Inside	$30.01	$30.02	$30.03
NBBO			2,000 shares		2,000 shares		
Exchange A	1,000 shares	1,000 shares	100 shares HFT / 900 shares institutional		1,000 shares	1,000 shares	500 shares
Exchange B	500 shares	500 shares	1,000 shares		1,000 shares	500 shares	500 shares

takes out top-of-book Exch A

Sell 1000 at 30.00

3. HFT detects potential adverse sweep selection – HFT looks to exit risk rather than exiting for edge at midpoint or better.
4. HFT submits "hide and light" sell 100 at 30.00 on Exchange A.
   4.1. HFT order locks NBBO (Exchange B still 30.00 bid for 1000); so HFT order is accepted and posted in a hidden state sell 100 at 30.00 on Exchange A.

HFT Sell hidden; locks NBBO

	$29.98	$29.99	$30.00	Inside	$30.01	$30.02	$30.03
NBBO			1,000 shares		2,000 shares		
Exchange A	1,000 shares	1,000 shares	Sell 100 shares HFT hidden	Inside	1,000 shares	1,000 shares	500 shares
Exchange B	500 shares	500 shares	1,000 shares		1,000 shares	500 shares	500 shares

Potential outcomes:

- Case 1: Institution joins NBBO on Exchange A with 30.00 bid for 100. This steps on HFT hidden order sell 100 at 30.00, providing HFT with flip out at scratch. HFT collects rebate on both legs of the trade.

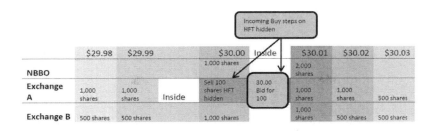

- Case 2: Incoming marketable order 30.01 bid for 100 on Exchange A. Per exchange rules, incoming order is matched with HFT order at midpoint 30.005. HFT flips out for half tick winner. HFT collects rebate on both legs of the trade.

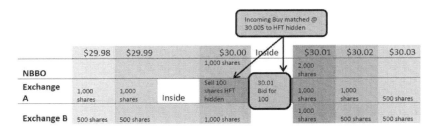

- Case 3: Away markets begin to fade. HFT flips out for scratch by hitting 30.00 bid on Exchange B while cancelling the hidden sell order on Exchange A. HFT collects one maker rebate but pays one taker fee. The taker fee is the "insurance cost" for this round trip trade.

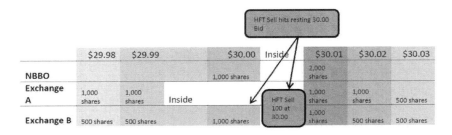

- Case 4: Away markets fade. HFT hidden sell order lights @ 30.00. HFT order is at top-of-queue top-of-book due to "hide and light" properties. HFT potentially flips out at scratch, collecting rebate on both legs of the trade, but holds execution risk (chance of fill < 100%). If order not filled, HFT potentially must flip out for loser.

	$29.98	$29.99	Inside	$30.00	$30.01	$30.02	$30.03
NBBO		1,500 shares		100 shares			
Exchange A	1,000 shares	1,000 shares		Sell 100 shares HFT lit	1,000 shares	1,000 shares	500 shares
Exchange B	500 shares	500 shares		1,000 shares	500 shares	500 shares	

HFT Sell order lights at top-of-queue top-of-book

Cases 1 and 2 are clear HFT winners even though this example is for an impending sweep event. Case 3 loses when the taker fee exceeds the maker rebate, but can be a winner if the flip out is done on an inverted "taker-maker" exchange, where the HFT is paid a taker rebate. Case 4 is a clear winner if the sell at 30.00 executes, otherwise is a loser.

In this simple example, it can be argued that losses due to cases 3 and 4 make the expected value of the round trip trade negative. However, given 13 exchanges and approximately 50 dark pools, there are a significant number of exit permutations, special order types and exchange features that serve as alternatives to insurance cost (case 3) or execution risk (case 4). Low latency, a prerequisite of successful HFT scalping, reduces the instances where the HFT is forced to trade on exchanges with less favorable economics in case 3 or into losing trades in case 4.

Appendix C: REG-NMS, Rule 610

Regulation NMS, Rule 610 – "The Market Access Rule" (570)

242.610 Access to quotations.

(a) <u>Quotations of SRO trading facility</u>. A national securities exchange or national securities association shall not impose unfairly discriminatory terms that prevent or inhibit any person from obtaining efficient access through a member of the national securities exchange or national securities association to the quotations in an NMS stock displayed through its SRO trading facility.

(b) <u>Quotations of SRO display-only facility</u>.

(1) Any trading center that displays quotations in an NMS stock through an SRO display-only facility shall provide a level and cost of access to such quotations that is substantially equivalent to the level and cost of access to quotations displayed by SRO trading facilities in that stock.

(2) Any trading center that displays quotations in an NMS stock through an SRO display-only facility shall not impose unfairly discriminatory terms that prevent or inhibit any person from obtaining efficient access to such quotations through a member, subscriber, or customer of the trading center.

(c) <u>Fees for access to quotations</u>. A trading center shall not impose, nor permit to be imposed, any fee or fees for the execution of an order against a protected quotation of the trading center or against any other quotation of the trading center that is the best bid or best offer of a national securities exchange, the best bid or best offer of The Nasdaq Stock Market, Inc., or the best bid or best offer of a national securities association other than the best bid or best offer of The Nasdaq Stock Market, Inc. in an NMS stock that exceed or accumulate to more than the following limits:

(1) If the price of a protected quotation or other quotation is $1.00 or more, the fee or fees cannot exceed or accumulate to more than $0.003 per share; or

(2) If the price of a protected quotation or other quotation is less than $1.00, the fee or fees cannot exceed or accumulate to more than 0.3% of the quotation price per share.

(d) Locking or crossing quotations. Each national securities exchange and national securities association shall establish, maintain, and enforce written rules that:

(1) Require its members reasonably to avoid:

(i) Displaying quotations that lock or cross any protected quotation in an NMS stock; and

(ii) Displaying manual quotations that lock or cross any quotation in an NMS stock disseminated pursuant to an effective national market system plan;

(2) Are reasonably designed to assure the reconciliation of locked or crossed quotations in an NMS stock; and

(3) Prohibit its members from engaging in a pattern or practice of displaying quotations that lock or cross any protected quotation in an NMS stock, or of displaying manual quotations that lock or cross any quotation in an NMS stock disseminated pursuant to an effective national market system plan, other than displaying quotations that lock or cross any protected or other quotation as permitted by an exception contained in its rules established pursuant to paragraph (d)(1) of this section.

(e) Exemptions. The Commission, by order, may exempt from the provisions of this section, either unconditionally or on specified terms and conditions, any person, security, quotations, orders, or fees, or any class or classes of persons, securities, quotations, orders, or fees, if the Commission determines that such exemption is necessary or appropriate in the public interest, and is consistent with the protection of investors.

http://www.sec.gov/rules/final/34-51808.pdf

Appendix D: REG-NMS, Rule 611

242.611 Order protection rule.

(a) <u>Reasonable policies and procedures</u>.

(1) A trading center shall establish, maintain, and enforce written policies and procedures that are reasonably designed to prevent trade-throughs on that trading center of protected quotations in NMS stocks that do not fall within an exception set forth in paragraph (b) of this section and, if relying on such an exception, that are reasonably designed to assure compliance with the terms of the exception.

(2) A trading center shall regularly surveil to ascertain the effectiveness of the policies and procedures required by paragraph (a)(1) of this section and shall take prompt action to remedy deficiencies in such policies and procedures.

(b) <u>Exceptions</u>.

(1) The transaction that constituted the trade-through was effected when the trading center displaying the protected quotation that was traded through was experiencing a failure, material delay, or malfunction of its systems or equipment.

(2) The transaction that constituted the trade-through was not a "regular way" contract.

(3) The transaction that constituted the trade-through was a single-priced opening, reopening, or closing transaction by the trading center.

(4) The transaction that constituted the trade-through was executed at a time when a protected bid was priced higher than a protected offer in the NMS stock.

(5) The transaction that constituted the trade-through was the execution of an order identified as an intermarket sweep order.

(6) The transaction that constituted the trade-through was effected by a trading center that simultaneously routed an intermarket sweep order to execute against the full displayed

size of any protected quotation in the NMS stock that was traded through.

(7) The transaction that constituted the trade-through was the execution of an order at a price that was not based, directly or indirectly, on the quoted price of the NMS stock at the time of execution and for which the material terms were not reasonably determinable at the time the commitment to execute the order was made.

(8) The trading center displaying the protected quotation that was traded through had displayed, within one second prior to execution of the transaction that constituted the trade-through, a best bid or best offer, as applicable, for the NMS stock with a price that was equal or inferior to the price of the trade-through transaction.

(9) The transaction that constituted the trade-through was the execution by a trading center of an order for which, at the time of receipt of the order, the trading center had guaranteed an execution at no worse than a specified price (a "stopped order"), where:

(i) The stopped order was for the account of a customer;

(ii) The customer agreed to the specified price on an order-by-order basis; and

(iii) The price of the trade-through transaction was, for a stopped buy order, lower than the national best bid in the NMS stock at the time of execution or, for a stopped sell order, higher than the national best offer in the NMS stock at the time of execution.

(c) Intermarket sweep orders. The trading center, broker, or dealer responsible for the routing of an intermarket sweep order shall take reasonable steps to establish that such order meets the requirements set forth in § 242.600(b)(30).

(d) Exemptions. The Commission, by order, may exempt from the provisions of this section, either unconditionally or on specified terms and conditions, any person, security, transaction, quotation, or order, or any class or classes of persons, securities, quotations, or orders, if the Commission determines that such exemption is necessary or appropriate in the public interest, and is consistent with the protection of investors.

http://www.sec.gov/rules/final/34-51808.pdf